Lent

with the
Desert Fathers

Thomas McKenzie

for Laura

*Jesus remained in the desert for forty days,
being tempted by Satan.
He was with the wild beasts;
and the angels ministered on him.*

Mark 1:13

© 2019, Thomas McKenzie
www.ThomasMcKenzie.com
Thomas@ThomasMcKenzie.com
Nashville, Tennessee

ISBN: 978-0-9960499-3-1

Scripture quotations marked (NIV) are taken from the Holy Bible, New International Version®, NIV®. Copyright © 1973, 1978, 1984, 2011 by Biblica, Inc.™ Used by permission of Zondervan. All rights reserved worldwide. www.zondervan.com The "NIV" and "New International Version" are trademarks registered in the United States Patent and Trademark Office by Biblica, Inc.™

Editing by E. H. McKenzie.

Quotations from the Desert Fathers are from the Vitae Patrum (Latin Text, 1628), and translated by Benedict Baker and Thomas McKenzie.

Cover design and photograph by Thomas McKenzie.

Table of Contents

Introduction

In the *Book of Common Prayer*, the priest begins the Ash Wednesday service by saying these words:

> Dear People of God: The first Christians observed with great devotion the days of our Lord's passion and resurrection, and it became the custom of the Church to prepare for them by a season of penitence and fasting. This season of Lent provided a time in which converts to the faith were prepared for Holy Baptism. It was also a time when those who, because of notorious sins, had been separated from the body of the faithful were reconciled by penitence and forgiveness, and restored to the fellowship of the Church. Thereby, the whole congregation was put in mind of the message of pardon and absolution set forth in the Gospel of our Savior, and of the need which all Christians continually have to renew their repentance and faith.
>
> I invite you, therefore, in the name of the Church, to the observance of a holy Lent, by self-examination and repentance; by prayer, fasting, and self-denial; and by reading and meditating on God's holy Word. And, to make a right beginning of repentance, and as a mark of our mortal nature, let us now kneel before the Lord, our maker and redeemer.

The Book of Common Prayer (1979), pg. 264

What is Lent?

Lent is a season of the Christian year. The purpose of Lent is not self-punishment. Jesus took all necessary punishment for our sins on the cross. We don't participate in Lent because we must. No one can (or should) make you enter Lent. You don't get extra points with God. Lent isn't even about becoming a better person. That isn't in our control, and only pride allows us to believe otherwise. No, Lent is about laying down some of our defenses and giving ourselves an opportunity to be formed by God. As in a desert we are unusually vulnerable to nature, so in Lent we are unusually vulnerable to the Lord.

The first day of Lent is Ash Wednesday. On this day, many churches offer people the chance to kneel and receive the "mark of our mortal nature." Palms from the previous year's Palm Sunday have been gathered, burned, and turned into ashes. The priest puts this ash on your forehead in the sign of a cross while saying, "Remember that you are dust, and to dust you shall return." The ashes remind us that even our greatest victories fail, and that all of our glory is destined for the trash bin. We are made of the basic elements of the universe: the dirt and the dust. What we are made of, we'll return to. Ash Wednesday sets the tone for the rest of this holy season.

During Lent, we take on spiritual disciplines. We give something up (sweets, alcohol, television, social media, etc.), or we take something on (serving the poor, extra financial giving, a devotional book, etc.). The disciplines are meant to empty us so that the Lord may fill us. We are making ourselves available to Christ in hope of growing in our faith. Lent is a time of preparation for Easter and Resurrection life. Lent focuses on Jesus' self-giving, his suffering, and his death. Lent is our desert.

Lent lasts for forty days, which are counted in an odd way. If you don't include Sundays as part of the season, Lent begins on Ash Wednesday and ends on Easter Sunday. That's because Sunday is always a feast day, a day to celebrate the Lord's resurrection, and people don't need to maintain their Lenten disciplines on Sundays. Lent ends at sunrise on Easter morning. People who count Lent this way often don't fast on Sunday. This is the more common way to think of Lent. The other way is to start on Ash Wednesday and count each and every day, including the Sundays. This makes Lent end a week before Easter, on Palm Sunday. Either way, this book has a chapter for every day from Ash Wednesday to Easter Sunday. That's a total of forty-seven days.

Who were the Desert Fathers?

In this Lent, you'll hear from the Desert Fathers. You may not be familiar with them. Most Christians aren't. A thousand years ago, they were the rock stars of the Church. Unfortunately, they've largely disappeared from our thoughts today.

The Desert Fathers lived in the 2nd-4th centuries A.D. They first dwelt in the deserts of Egypt, but later they could be found in modern-day Israel, Jordan, and Syria. In those days, Northern Egypt, and especially the great city of Alexandria, was a center of Christianity. The first wave of Fathers were Christian men and women who left the safety of their homes and moved into the desert. (Oddly enough, the word "Father" in this context can be mean a man or a woman.) Many lived alone, though communities also developed.

Essentially, the Desert Fathers were people who wanted to know God more fully, and they were willing to do anything for that to happen. There are many fascinating stories of their lives and adventures. Some of these tales are intense, some are disturbing, and some can be hard to believe. Whether all the stories are true we don't know. We do know, however, that many Fathers were filled with deep, godly wisdom. Thankfully, many of their words were preserved by others who knew them.

The wisdom of the Desert Fathers was often recorded in short sayings, which were called "Words." The book you're holding features 47 of those words. Out of the hundreds available, I prayerfully chose these because I thought they would be most helpful to my readers during their Lenten journey. If you'd like to read more, or learn more about the Desert Fathers, I have a bibliography at the end of this book.

Entering the Desert

Following Jesus Christ is, from one perspective, impossible. After all, where is he? I've never seen him. I've never heard him teach the crowds. I didn't see him walk on water. I've never felt the nail holes in his hands. I've certainly never walked in his footsteps.

Following Jesus Christ is, from another perspective, miraculous. Having been raised from the dead, he ascended into Heaven. Reigning from Heaven, he also fills all things. He is in every person, every thing, and every empty space. In the words of the Bible, he "fills all things" (Ephesians 1:23). He is closer to us than anyone or anything else could ever be. The call to follow him still rings out over deserts and mountains, valleys and seas, and in the quiet of our minds and hearts. Hearing that call and choosing to obey is a miracle. We cannot literally walk in Jesus' footsteps. But, by his grace, we can follow his lead.

Three of the four Gospel books tell us that Jesus fasted for forty days in the Palestinian desert. Since then, Christians have followed him into our own deserts. Some of those deserts are literally sandy, hot, and dry. Others are deserts of the soul. Sometimes, we stumble into these deserts unintentionally. We're living our lives just fine, and then, suddenly, we're lost. Tragedy, death, sickness, disaster, or betrayal upend our lives. We wake up in a desert of chaos. Other times, we go to the desert on purpose. Some of us do that physically. But even if we don't actually go to dry lands, we can still walk into the desert.

A non-physical desert is a time of dryness. It's a time when those things upon which we usually rely simply aren't there. Accidental deserts come from loss of relationships, jobs, health, or other important aspects of our lives. Intentional deserts are usually less stressful. We enter them when we fast from certain pleasures or take on new disciplines.

While deserts are painful, they can also be helpful. They mould and shape the soul. The Church, noticing that we all need occasional time in the desert, invented Lent. In this holy season, we symbolically follow Jesus into the desert. The entire Christian community, worldwide, is invited. Catholics and Protestants, Orthodox and Pentecostal, Liberals and Fundamentalists—we're all welcome to this inner pilgrimage. We begin on Ash Wednesday, and we end with Good Friday and Easter Sunday. In between, we follow in

Jesus' footsteps through prayer, fasting, contemplation, reading, giving, and self-denial.

Hearing Voices

I spend at least one week per year in a physical desert, one in Northern New Mexico. I stay at the Monastery of Christ in the Desert. From time to time, I bring a few men with me. After the first day there, the thing on which these men most always comment is the silence. There's no TV, phone or internet. When people talk, which isn't often, they speak in low voices.

Deserts are quiet places, even symbolic deserts like Lent. When we practice Lent, we shut down some of our normal distractions. This leads to a kind of inner silence.

When we're silent, we begin to hear voices that we don't normally hear. I think those voices are always present, but they can be hard to pick up when we're surrounded by noise. There are three voices I notice in those quiet places: my voice, God's voice, and the Devil's voice. I notice myself, my creative thoughts, but also my sinful desires. I more easily hear from the Lord, but I also hear from the Devil.

When I read the Desert Fathers, it's clear to me that they had the same kind of experiences. Many of their stories have to do with hearing those three voices. When you enter into the desert of Lent, I feel fairly sure you'll hear those voices, too. Don't be surprised if you do.

How to Use this Book

The purpose of this book is to help guide you through Lent. There's a little chapter for each day. It's recommended that you set aside five minutes a day to read and consider the chapter. You might find it helpful to do this first thing in the morning, maybe just before breakfast or with your coffee. That way, you'll hopefully start the day off on the right foot.

A moment of silence is a great way to begin. Each chapter then starts with a quotation from the "Vitae Patrum," a collection of the sayings of the Desert Fathers. These words establish the theme of the day. Next, you'll find some thoughts on the theme. After the comments, there's a scripture verse to read and consider. You'll also find a suggested action. These actions really are just suggestions. They are simple ways to engage a bit more fully in Lent. It's recommended that you end each chapter with the Lord's Prayer.

Good News

My one great fear in writing this book is that a reader will get a message that is entirely untrue. That message is this: "If I am spiritual enough, God will accept me." Here's how that could happen. The Desert Fathers were intense. Seriously intense. These are people who spent their entire lives devoted to prayer in some of the most inhospitable places on Earth. Much of what they say isn't about God's love. Most of it is about how we should live.

I believe the reason that most of these sayings are not explicitly about God's love is that the Fathers *assumed* it. They knew the Holy Spirit personally. Jesus Christ was revealed to them in prayer, labor, nature, and sacraments. I have no doubt these men and women were close to the God who calls himself "love" (1st John 4:8). These short sayings, on the other hand, are words of advice to those who want to know God better. They are sober and practical, not mushy or ethereal.

The same is true of the actions I suggest in each chapter. I'm hoping to give the reader a way to live some of this wisdom in real life. I'm not trying to burden anyone.

You are accepted by God not because of what you do, or say, or feel. You are accepted because of what Jesus Christ did for you. God became a man, taught us how to live, performed miracles, gave us the Church and the sacraments, and then died for us. He came back from the dead, ascended into heaven, and sent his Holy Spirit. Right now, he is near you and is simultaneously praying to the Father for you. There is nothing you have to do to prove yourself to God. Rather, he comes to you and asks that you trust him. He even gives you the grace to trust him. As you trust him, he brings you into himself.

If you never read this book, never do anything suggested in it, never pray any of these prayers, and ignore everything here, God still loves you and accepts you in Christ. You don't need to live alone in the desert to know God. He knows you and loves you as you are. The words of the Desert Fathers might help you in your life, or they might not. Jesus is greater than anything in this book.

How to Locate the Date of Ash Wednesday This Year

Lent begins on Ash Wednesday. If you know what day Ash Wednesday is this year, you can easily follow this book. Unfortunately, Ash Wednesday is on a different day every year.

If you are part of a tradition that celebrates Lent, then your church will let you know when Ash Wednesday is. If you're not, then simply search "when is Ash Wednesday." The answer will magically appear.

It is far easier to walk through Lent within the context of a Christian congregation that is doing the same thing. If you aren't already part of a church, denominations that normally practice Lent are Roman Catholics, Anglicans, Methodists, Episcopalians, Lutherans and sometimes Presbyterians. Eastern Orthodox also practice Lent, but they may or may not have an Ash Wednesday. If you're Orthodox, simply ask your priest how to incorporate this book into your tradition.

Ash Wednesday

Begin with a moment of silence.

A Word from Saint Syncletica, a Mother of the desert.

Amma Syncletica said, "There is immense labor and strife for the sinner who turns to God, but afterwards unspeakable joy. If you are trying to light a fire, before you succeed you get smothered in smoke, which irritates and brings tears to the eyes. Just so, it is written that our God is a consuming fire, and it is fitting that the divine fire should be lit in ourselves with tears and hard work."

Reflection on today's Word.

This is the first day of Lent, and your first day of reading this devotional book. It may also be your last day for both. I get that. Taking on something "spiritual" sounds like a good idea. You know you "need to do it." But, if you're anything like me, your intended-self is far more disciplined that your real-life-self.

As Syncletica points out in our Word, getting started on something spiritual (like Lent) is painful. It's like starting a campfire. At first, all you get is smoke in your eyes. The fire keeps going out, and you get frustrated. But if you stick with it, if you persist, if you call out to God for help, a fire begins to blaze. And then you get to make s'mores.

Keep going. Pick a discipline you can do, like reading this book every day. Also, give something up. Make some space in your life. For me, I usually delete games from my phone. For you it might be chocolate, beer, cursing, or whatever. Pick something, decided to put it away for 40 days, and then tell someone. Having a buddy can really help.

Ask God to help you. He will. For whatever reason, he led you to this book. He must have something for you this Lent. Give him the space to reach your heart. He has work to do.

An action you might take today, in order to put the Word into practice.

Choose something to give up for Lent, and then tell one other person about what you're doing. Give them permission to ask you about how it's going.

Consider today's Bible passage: Mark 2:14 (NIV)

As he walked along, Jesus saw Levi son of Alphaeus working in a toll booth. "Follow me," Jesus told him, and Levi got up and followed him.

Conclude with the Lord's Prayer.

Our Father, who art in heaven,
hallowed be thy Name,
thy kingdom come,
thy will be done,
on earth as it is in heaven.
Give us this day our daily bread.
And forgive us our trespasses,
as we forgive those
who trespass against us.
And lead us not into temptation,
but deliver us from evil.
For thine is the kingdom,
and the power, and the glory,
for ever and ever. Amen.

The Thursday after Ash Wednesday

Begin with a moment of silence.

A Word from St. Anthony the Great, a Father of the desert.

Abba Anthony said, "Don't put your trust in your own righteousness, don't fixate on the past, and watch over your tongue and belly."

Reflection on today's Word.

When I started reading the Desert Fathers, I was surprised by how many times they make bold assertions. Today's statement from Anthony is a good example. What is he talking about? Why does he care so much about three things which seem kind of odd and unrelated?

I think some context here will be helpful. In this ancient world, younger people would sometimes come to an older, wiser person in the faith and ask for "a Word." What they meant was "give me an insight that will help my life." The older person would then share a bit of wisdom. That bit of wisdom was meant for that specific younger person, and might not be applicable to everyone. In fact, the Fathers would sometimes say contradictory things to different people.

This saying from Abba Anthony is such a "Word." All three parts of this Word speak directly to me. The first part is "don't trust in your own righteousness." I'm always doing that. I can be judgmental, thinking that I'm better than other people. I think "if I were in that situation, I wouldn't have done that bad thing." Of course, I have no idea what I would have done. When I judge others, I'm trusting in my own righteousness.

Anthony tells us not to fixate on the past. That's a hard one. I naturally worry about the past. I feel guilt and shame about past misdeeds, and I resent people who've hurt me. I know I need God's help with this.

My tongue and my belly both get me into trouble. I say stupid, hurtful, thoughtless things. I also overeat, to the detriment of my long-term health. Anthony has me pegged on this one, too.

What would a word to you sound like? What would an Abba say to you today? Is there some specific advice you think you need to hear?

An action you might take today, in order to put the Word into practice.

Consider what specific direction a wise person would give you today, like "be kind," or "forgive yourself." Then ask the Lord to help you with that specific direction today.

Consider today's Bible passage: Luke 18:18-22 (NIV)

A certain ruler asked him, "Good teacher, what must I do to inherit eternal life?" "Why do you call me good?" Jesus answered. "No one is good— except God alone. You know the commandments: 'You shall not commit adultery, you shall not murder, you shall not steal, you shall not give false testimony, honor your father and mother.' "All these I have kept since I was a boy," he said. When Jesus heard this, he said to him, "You still lack one thing. Sell everything you have and give to the poor, and you will have treasure in heaven. Then come, follow me."

Conclude with the Lord's Prayer.

Our Father, who art in heaven,
hallowed be thy Name,
thy kingdom come,
thy will be done,
on earth as it is in heaven.
Give us this day our daily bread.
And forgive us our trespasses,
as we forgive those
who trespass against us.
And lead us not into temptation,
but deliver us from evil.
For thine is the kingdom,
and the power, and the glory,
for ever and ever. Amen.

The Friday after Ash Wednesday

Begin with a moment of silence.

A Word from Poemon, a Father of the desert, to his disciple, Ammon.

Abba Ammon asked Abba Poemon about the unclean thoughts and desires of Ammon's heart. Abba Poemen replied, "Does the axe claim more credit that the man who wields it? If you weren't striving against these thoughts, you wouldn't have any work to do."

Reflection on today's Word.

Last summer, I decided to chop down a tree. The tree was dead and just taking up space in my backyard. I could have borrowed my friend's chainsaw, but I thought it would be cool to use an axe. I thought it would be good exercise, and kind of manly. So, I bought an axe.

Let's just say it wasn't as great as I thought it would be. It took forever, and was really difficult. My shoulders ached for days, and my hands went numb for hours. When the tree finally came down, it left a large, tall, jagged stump. Then I still had a dead tree to chop up and haul out of my yard. And the stump is still there.

In our reading today, Poemon compares dealing with unclean thoughts to using an axe. It's painful, sweaty, messy work; and the results aren't as clean as you would hope. Even worse, there's always more to do. A fallen tree still has to be cut to pieces. When that's done, there's always another tree to cut down. It never ends.

Unclean thoughts and desires are like unwanted trees. Like nasty, quickly growing, sticky, thorny, hard trees. Once you start chopping, you'll be chopping at them your whole life. There's no end to the work. But Poemon is telling us that this is OK. That's the human condition. And the work is important. The work strengthens us. The work is glorifying to the Lord and a blessing to us and those we love. The work has good results, even if it can be painful and depressing. Yes, God will help us when we call out to him, but the work is still ours. So pray for his grace, and keep your axe swinging.

An action you might take today, in order to put the Word into practice.

What tree needs to be cut down in your life? Is there a habit, a destructive relationship, or a way of thinking that is getting in your way? How can you chop some of it down today?

Consider today's Bible passage: Joshua 1:9 (NIV)

The Lord said to Joshua, "Have I not commanded you? Be strong and courageous. Do not be afraid; do not be discouraged, for the Lord your God will be with you wherever you go."

Conclude with the Lord's Prayer.

Our Father, who art in heaven,
hallowed be thy Name,
thy kingdom come,
thy will be done,
on earth as it is in heaven.
Give us this day our daily bread.
And forgive us our trespasses,
as we forgive those
who trespass against us.
And lead us not into temptation,
but deliver us from evil.
For thine is the kingdom,
and the power, and the glory,
for ever and ever. Amen.

The Saturday After Ash Wednesday

Begin with a moment of silence.

A Word from Sisois, a Father of the desert, to one of his disciples.

A disciple said to Abba Sisois, "I would love to be able to keep guard over my heart." Sisois replied, "How can you keep guard over your heart if your mouth is like an open door?"

Reflection on today's Word.

Sometimes the thing that I think is "the problem" isn't really the problem. I might think my problem is the traffic, or my boss's incompetence, or my spouse's mood. Those things can certainly be difficult for me. But the real problem in my life is most often me.

In today's Word, the disciple wants to protect his inner self. He's concerned that bad things are coming in from the outside, and he need's advice from Sisois. Sisois is not so worried about things that come from the outside in, he's much more concerned about bad stuff that comes from the inside and gets out. That's why he suggests the disciple pay attention to what's coming out of his own mouth.

An action you might take today, in order to put the Word into practice.

Pay special attention to your words today. Ask the Lord's help to say things that are loving, helpful, and true.

Consider today's Bible passage: Luke 6:45 (NIV)

Jesus said, "A good man brings good things out of the good stored up in his heart, and an evil man brings evil things out of the evil stored up in his heart. For the mouth speaks what the heart is full of."

Conclude with the Lord's Prayer.

The First Sunday in Lent

Begin with a moment of silence.

A Word from Macarius, a Father of the desert.

Abba Macarius said, "There is no need for many words in prayer. Just stretch out your hands from time to time and say, 'Lord as you will and as you know, have mercy upon me.' And if conflict arises in your heart say, 'Help.' The Lord knows your needs, and he will have mercy upon you."

Reflection on today's Word.

I'm a pastor, so people often ask me about prayer. They're often afraid because they don't want to "do it wrong." There are many books of prayers that people cay buy. These books are meant to teach us what to say to God, sometimes with the implicit idea that saying our prayers correctly will get us what we want or need. Unfortunately, I have seen a great deal of anxiety expressed by people who simply want to pray, but don't want to mess it up.

How we pray is not really the issue. Even what we pray might not be as important as we think it is. I think the real trick is to pray *at all*. God knows us far better than we know ourselves, and he knows what's going on in us. I wish folks would not worry about what to say, or how to say it. Instead, we can simply call out to him. Literally, just speak the words "God, I need you." That's Macarius' message today. Even though he likely spent many hours a day in prayer, he knew the best prayers are simple, with few words but with heartfelt intention.

An action you might take today, in order to put the Word into practice.

Whatever you experience today, tell the Lord about it. If something good happens, tell him "thank you." If something bad happens, ask him to help you.

Consider today's Bible passage: Luke 18:9-14 (NIV)

To some who were confident of their own righteousness and looked down on everyone else, Jesus told this parable: "Two men went up to the temple to pray, one a Pharisee and the other a tax collector. The Pharisee stood by himself and prayed: 'God, I thank you that I am not like other people—robbers, evildoers, adulterers—or even like this tax collector. I fast twice a week and give a tenth of all I get.'

"But the tax collector stood at a distance. He would not even look up to heaven, but beat his breast and said, 'God, have mercy on me, a sinner.'

"I tell you that this man, rather than the other, went home justified before God. For all those who exalt themselves will be humbled, and those who humble themselves will be exalted."

Conclude with the Lord's Prayer.

Our Father, who art in heaven,
hallowed be thy Name,
thy kingdom come,
thy will be done,
on earth as it is in heaven.
Give us this day our daily bread.
And forgive us our trespasses,
as we forgive those
who trespass against us.
And lead us not into temptation,
but deliver us from evil.
For thine is the kingdom,
and the power, and the glory,
for ever and ever. Amen.

A Word about Sundays

This book is meant to guide you through Lent as an individual. However, you aren't alone as a Christian. You are one of over two billion of us in the world today. Rather than be alone in your faith today, please attend a worship service at a local church. If you don't normally attend church, consider finding one that preaches the Good News of Jesus and celebrates Communion on Sundays. If you can't attend church due to illness or incapacity, reach out to your church. See if they can visit you and bring you Communion.

Monday after the First Sunday in Lent

Begin with a moment of silence.

A Word from St. Anthony the Great, a Father of the desert.

When Abba Anthony was asked, "What rule should I keep in order to please God?" the abba replied, "Follow this rule which I give you. Wherever you go, keep God continually before your eyes. Follow Holy Scripture in everything you do. Wherever you happen to be, don't try to move on too quickly. Do these three things and you will live."

Reflection on today's Word.

Disciples of the Desert Fathers often asked the them for a rule. By "rule" they didn't mean so much a law, but rather, a path. What path should I take? All of the Fathers point us to Jesus as the true path, of course. But how we walk with Jesus will vary depending on our life circumstances.

In this case, Abba Anthony recommends three attributes of a good path. The first is that we should remember God. Unfortunately, God can be easy to forget. Because we don't see him, he can fade into the background. Our lives are so filled with distractions that we can unintentionally lose track of the most important person in the universe. Doing what we can to remember the Lord is important. I have an alarm set on my watch that reminds me to say the Lord's Prayer seven times a day. That helps me remember God.

The second rule is that we should read, meditate on, and be guided by the Bible. That seems reasonable. The Bible is God's Word, after all. In it, we find everything we need for salvation. That's why this book has daily Bible readings, along with the Words from the Fathers. Reading God's Word is an important daily practice.

The third principle is that we should not be too quick to move or change. While those first two principles might be obvious, the third is less so. Why does Anthony say that this is an important part of the Christian path?

God often reveals himself in difficulty. When difficulties happen, one response that many people have is to run away. We think that a new job, a new romantic partner, or a new apartment will make everything OK. As a friend of mine says, "We seek geographical solutions to non-geographical problems." Most of the time, we come to realize that "wherever you go, there you are." Our problems aren't often external. Most of them are based in what's going on in our hearts.

If you are in difficulty, don't run away quickly. Assuming you aren't in danger, let the hard thing happen and live with it. Ask the Lord for patience. See if God doesn't have something for you in the midst of it.

An action you might take today, in order to put the Word into practice.

What trouble do you want to run from today? Instead, pray that God will reveal himself in that trouble (unless you are in danger; then, get going).

Consider today's Bible passage: 2 Samuel 22:2-4 (NIV)

The Lord is my rock, my fortress and my deliverer;
    my God is my rock, in whom I take refuge,
    my shield and the horn of my salvation.
He is my stronghold, my refuge and my savior—
    from violent people you save me.
I called to the Lord, who is worthy of praise,
    and have been saved from my enemies.

Conclude with the Lord's Prayer.

Our Father, who art in heaven,
hallowed be thy Name,
thy kingdom come,
thy will be done,
on earth as it is in heaven.
Give us this day our daily bread.
And forgive us our trespasses,
as we forgive those
who trespass against us.
And lead us not into temptation,
but deliver us from evil.
For thine is the kingdom,
and the power, and the glory,
for ever and ever. Amen.

Tuesday after the First Sunday in Lent

Begin with a moment of silence.

A Word from Pambo to his friends, when he came to the great city to visit his Bishop, St. Athanasius the Great.

Athanasius asked Abba Pambo to come down to Alexandria from the desert. When Pambo arrived he saw a woman of the theater, and wept. Asked by his companions why he wept he said, "Two things move me. First that this woman is lost, and secondly that I myself have not tried to please God half as much as this woman has tried to satisfy the desires of men."

Reflection on today's Word.

I once received an invitation to speak at a well-known church in England. The invitation came with a promise to fly me there, take care of my expenses, and pay me a speaking fee. I was thrilled. I love to travel, I could use the money, and it made me feel great. But then I started to ask myself "why?" Why would they want me, specifically? After doing some research, I found out that this was a scam. Whoever wrote that email had gone through a lot of trouble to make it look legitimate, but all they really wanted was to get access to my bank account.

It's amazing how much research and creativity went into that scam! I wondered what might happen if this criminal put the same effort into a legitimate business. They might do very well for themselves.

In the Word for today, Abba Pambo sees a "woman of the theater." In his world, theater was often associated with immoral behavior. In our context, we might think of this woman as an exotic dancer or prostitute.

Remember that Pambo rarely sees women at all, and may not have seen a woman like this in decades. He has a strong and unusual emotional reaction to her. For one thing, he's worried for her soul. He knows God loves everyone, including this woman. He also knows that God wants a better life for her, both in the present and in eternity.

But Pambo also sees how hard she's working. She's putting a great deal of effort into pleasing her customers. While he doesn't agree with her profession, he's shamed by her industriousness. He's convicted that he should put that same amount of effort into pleasing God.
Even Pambo, who gave his entire life to the Lord, is humble enough to admit that he doesn't do enough. That's a good example for me. If my relationship with God is based on how much I do, I am in big trouble. Praise be to Jesus that he is faithful to me even when I'm not faithful to him.

An action you might take today, in order to put the Word into practice.

Put some energy into a specific action as an offering to God. Perhaps call someone you've been avoiding, or help someone in need. Ask God for the grace to put as much effort into his Kingdom as you usually put into other important things in your life.

Consider today's Bible passage: Mathew 21:28-32 (NIV)

Jesus said, "What do you think? There was a man who had two sons. He went to the first and said, 'Son, go and work today in the vineyard.'
"'I will not,' he answered, but later he changed his mind and went.
"Then the father went to the other son and said the same thing. He answered, 'I will, sir,' but he did not go.
"Which of the two did what his father wanted?"
"The first," they (the religious people) answered.

Jesus said to them, "Truly I tell you, the tax collectors and the prostitutes are entering the kingdom of God ahead of you. For John (the Baptizer) came to you to show you the way of righteousness, and you did not believe him, but the tax collectors and the prostitutes did. And even after you saw this, you did not repent and believe him.

Conclude with the Lord's Prayer.

Our Father, who art in heaven,
hallowed be thy Name,
thy kingdom come,
thy will be done,
on earth as it is in heaven.
Give us this day our daily bread.
And forgive us our trespasses,
as we forgive those
who trespass against us.
And lead us not into temptation,
but deliver us from evil.
For thine is the kingdom,
and the power, and the glory,
for ever and ever. Amen.

Wednesday after the First Sunday in Lent

Begin with a moment of silence.

A Word from the life of Sara, a Mother of the desert.

For thirteen years, Amma Sara was severely attacked by the demon of sexual temptation. She never prayed to be released from this battle, but only kept saying, "Lord give me strength."

Reflection on today's Word.

We're all sexual beings, and that's a good thing. That's part of who God made us to be. Sexuality is the body's longing for intimacy. We are created for intimacy, for deep communion with one another and, ultimately, with God. Unfortunately, in our society sexuality is deeply broken and commodified. It has digressed from intimacy to entertainment, and often to shame.

Sara's battle is common to all of us. We're each called to direct our sexual desire in godly ways. But our bodies, our hormones, and our minds can override our religious ideals. Amma Sara thought of this as a demon, and whether it was a literal demon or not doesn't really matter. Sexual temptation can be overwhelming.

Sara didn't even bother to ask to be free of that temptation. She probably knew she wouldn't be. After all, sex is part of humanity. Instead she went to the Lord and asked for strength. That's the best thing any of us can do, in any kind of temptation. The Lord alone can help us. Even if we do resist temptation in our own strength, that would just make us proud and lead us to rely on ourselves. Self-reliance, also known as pride, is quite dangerous to the soul.

The amazing thing is that the Lord does help those who call upon him. When we're in need, when we are tempted, we can call out for help. It's amazing how God helps those who reach out to him.

An action you might take today, in order to put the word into practice.

At some point today, you will likely tempted to do something morally wrong. It might be a temptation to gossip, to judge, to retaliate, to steal, or any number of any things. When one of those temptations comes, close your eyes, take a deep breath, and ask the Lord for strength not to give in.

Consider today's Bible passage: 1st Corinthians 10:12-32 (NIV)

If you think you are standing firm, be careful that you don't fall! No temptation has overtaken you except what is common to mankind. And God is faithful; he will not let you be tempted beyond what you can bear. But when you are tempted, he will also provide a way out so that you can endure it.

Conclude with the Lord's Prayer.

Our Father, who art in heaven,
hallowed be thy Name,
thy kingdom come,
thy will be done,
on earth as it is in heaven.
Give us this day our daily bread.
And forgive us our trespasses,
as we forgive those
who trespass against us.
And lead us not into temptation,
but deliver us from evil.
For thine is the kingdom,
and the power, and the glory,
for ever and ever. Amen.

Thursday after the First Sunday in Lent

Begin with a moment of silence.

A Word from Poemen, a Father of the desert.

Abba Poemen said, "Whatever troubles you can be overcome by silence."

Reflection on today's Word.

If Abba Poemen were to show up today, he might think that Americans believe that "whatever troubles you can be avoided by noise." We live in a noisy world, and I'm not just referring to city traffic or airplanes flying overhead. I mean that we fill our lives with endless distraction. From the moment we get up in the morning until our heads hit the pillow at night, we have the TV on, we have music on, we're looking at our phones (sometimes all at the same time), and/or we're talking to someone. Some of us even have radios in our showers and TVs on our dining tables.

By continually allowing ourselves to be distracted by noise, we avoid our own thoughts and feelings. We're also avoiding God.

The prophet Elijah was once invited by God to a meeting. When he went, there were a series of dramatic events: a storm, an earthquake, and a fire. But God was not in these. Instead, he was in the "still, small voice" (1 Kings 19:12) that could only be heard in the silence.

Of course, God can break through any distractions. But the Bible shows us that we often encounter him in silence. I'm assuming you are reading this book because you want to encounter God. You want to hear from him, or at least to be in his presence. My best suggestion to you is to read the scriptures, and then be quiet. Put away the noise, if even for a few minutes. Allow God to have some space; allow your soul to have some time. Give yourself the blessing of a more quiet life this Lent.

An action you might take today, in order to put the Word into practice.

Spend some time in silence today. In a situation in which you would normally listen to music, or have the TV on, or look at your phone—don't. Be quiet, if only for five or ten minutes.

Consider today's Bible passage: 1st Kings 19:9b-13 (NIV)

And the word of the Lord came to him: "What are you doing here, Elijah?" He replied, "I have been very zealous for the Lord God Almighty. The Israelites have rejected your covenant, torn down your altars, and put your prophets to death with the sword. I am the only one left, and now they are trying to kill me too."

The Lord said, "Go out and stand on the mountain in the presence of the Lord, for the Lord is about to pass by."

Then a great and powerful wind tore the mountains apart and shattered the rocks before the Lord, but the Lord was not in the wind. After the wind there was an earthquake, but the Lord was not in the earthquake. After the earthquake came a fire, but the Lord was not in the fire. And after the fire came a gentle whisper. When Elijah heard it, he pulled his cloak over his face and went out and stood at the mouth of the cave.

Conclude with the Lord's Prayer.

Our Father, who art in heaven,
hallowed be thy Name,
thy kingdom come,
thy will be done,
on earth as it is in heaven.
Give us this day our daily bread.
And forgive us our trespasses,
as we forgive those
who trespass against us.
And lead us not into temptation,
but deliver us from evil.
For thine is the kingdom,
and the power, and the glory,
for ever and ever. Amen.

Friday after the First Sunday in Lent

Begin with a moment of silence.

A Word from an anonymous Mother or Father of the desert.

An abba said, "Anyone who is praised or honored above what he deserves runs a greater risk of being brought low. But he who has no reputation at all among men will in the end be lifted up."

Reflection on today's Word.

Several years ago, I read a report concerning pastors who had "fallen." These were mainly men (though there were a few women) who had broken the trust of their churches in a serious way. Many of them had had affairs, while others had stolen money or seriously misused their power.

Those who wrote the report interviewed a large number of former church leaders from many different backgrounds. They were looking for some commonality, some trait or flaw that all the pastors shared. They found one common thing. In each of the interviews, at some point, the former pastor said, "I never thought it could happen to me."

That was the key to their moral failure: they thought they were above it. Even though most pastors would theologically agree that all of us are sinners, that all of us are broken and capable of evil, somehow these men and women felt this was not really true of them. Why? Well, if they are anything like me it's because they started to "believe their own press," as the saying goes. In other words, they thought too highly of themselves.

This is what our Word is telling us today. If we are flattered by others, we run the risk of becoming prideful. We begin to believe that we really are what they say we are. On the other hand, if we humble ourselves, or if our circumstances humble us, our souls are in a better position. God lifts up the humble, but he brings down the prideful.

An action you might take today, in order to put the Word into practice.

What good things do people say about you? Which of these are not true, or are not as true as people think? Offer that difference to the Lord, and ask to have an honest view of yourself.

Consider today's Bible passage: Luke 14:7-11 (NIV)

When Jesus noticed how the guests picked the places of honor at the table, he told them this parable: "When someone invites you to a wedding feast, do not take the place of honor, for a person more distinguished than you may have been invited. If so, the host who invited both of you will come and say to you, 'Give this person your seat.' Then, humiliated, you will have to take the least important place. But when you are invited, take the lowest place, so that when your host comes, he will say to you, 'Friend, move up to a better place.' Then you will be honored in the presence of all the other guests. For all those who exalt themselves will be humbled, and those who humble themselves will be exalted."

Conclude with the Lord's Prayer.

Our Father, who art in heaven,
hallowed be thy Name,
thy kingdom come,
thy will be done,
on earth as it is in heaven.
Give us this day our daily bread.
And forgive us our trespasses,
as we forgive those
who trespass against us.
And lead us not into temptation,
but deliver us from evil.
For thine is the kingdom,
and the power, and the glory,
for ever and ever. Amen.

Saturday after the First Sunday in Lent

Begin with a moment of silence.

A Word from Evagrius, a hermit of the desert.

Abba Evagrius said, "The beginning of salvation is to distrust your own arguments."

Reflection on today's Word.

I spend too much time on social media. I sometimes engage in arguments on Facebook or Twitter. These almost never end well. Usually they just escalate into personal attacks, and then someone gets unfriended or blocked.

The other day, I was having one of those arguments with a friend of a friend, a guy I don't even know. I won't distract you by telling you what it was about, but it involved statistics. He brought up some numbers, and I countered with my own. We went back and forth, both of us apparently googling sites to back up our points of view. After a while, he did something truly extraordinary. He said he was wrong. After looking at the evidence, he saw that he had been mistaken and he was now in favor of the opposite opinion.

It's hard for human beings to change our minds. It's actually contrary to the way our brains work. In order to change our minds, we sometimes have to distrust our own understanding of reality. That is exactly what Evagrius is calling us to do today. If we're going to grow in Christ, we have to doubt our own brains. Why? Because all of us hold ideas and opinions that are contrary to Jesus and his Gospel. Only Jesus has all the truth. The rest of us only partially understand reality. Our progress in faith comes when we abandon our egos and submit to the truth of God and his Word.

An action you might take today, in order to put the Word into practice.

Ask God to show you one opinion or idea you have which is not in line with Jesus' teachings. Can you reconsider that opinion and change your mind?

Consider today's Bible passage: Romans 12:2 (NIV)

Do not conform to the pattern of this world, but be transformed by the renewing of your mind. Then you will be able to test and approve what God's will is—his good, pleasing and perfect will.

Conclude with the Lord's Prayer.

Our Father, who art in heaven,
hallowed be thy Name,
thy kingdom come,
thy will be done,
on earth as it is in heaven.
Give us this day our daily bread.
And forgive us our trespasses,
as we forgive those
who trespass against us.
And lead us not into temptation,
but deliver us from evil.
For thine is the kingdom,
and the power, and the glory,
for ever and ever. Amen

Tomorrow is Sunday

Plan to attend a worship service tomorrow. Attend your usual church, or a church nearby. Or visit a church you've been meaning to attend. If the church is also practicing Lent, all the better.

Second Sunday in Lent

Begin with a moment of silence.

A Word from a conversation between Poemen, a Father of the desert, and one of his disciples.

A disciple said to Abba Poemen, "There are many dangerous thoughts which come into my mind." Abba Poemen said, "Spread out your cloak and capture some wind for me." "It's not possible," the disciple replied. Poemen said "neither is it possible to prevent all kinds of thoughts coming in to your mind. What you can do is resist them."

Reflection on today's Word.

Some of the best folks to talk to are alcoholics who've been in recovery for a long time. They are wiser than most other people in the way they consider their own thoughts and actions.

A long-sober alcoholic I know would agree with Poemen's Word. He would tell you that there have been times when he's thought about drinking every minute of the day. Those thoughts come into his mind whether he wants them to or not.

How does he handle them? Today, he'll tell you that when the thought of drinking comes, he turns it into a prayer. "Thank you, God, that I don't need to drink right now." That simple action doesn't stop the thoughts, or make him a morally superior person, or take away his alcoholism. But the prayer does allow God to do something in his soul.

Ultimately, it isn't the thoughts of alcohol that are the problem. The problem is the drinking. God can keep him from drinking as he puts his trust in God alone, but even God doesn't stop the thoughts from coming. Thanks be to God for the help he gives when we ask for it.

An action you might take today, in order to put the Word into practice.

You will probably have a troubling thought today. When it happens, don't ignore it. Rather, turn it into a prayer.

Consider today's Bible passage: James 1:2-5 (NIV)

Consider it pure joy, my brothers and sisters, whenever you face trials of many kinds, because you know that the testing of your faith produces perseverance. Let perseverance finish its work so that you may be mature and complete, not lacking anything. If any of you lacks wisdom, you should ask God, who gives generously to all without finding fault, and it will be given to you.

Conclude with the Lord's Prayer.

Our Father, who art in heaven,
hallowed be thy Name,
thy kingdom come,
thy will be done,
on earth as it is in heaven.
Give us this day our daily bread.
And forgive us our trespasses,
as we forgive those
who trespass against us.
And lead us not into temptation,
but deliver us from evil.
For thine is the kingdom,
and the power, and the glory,
for ever and ever. Amen.

Today is Sunday

If you are a member of a church, please attend worship today. If not, visit a church. Churches can provide important community, especially as you are going through Lent.

Monday after the Second Sunday in Lent

Begin with a moment of silence.

A Word from St. Anthony the Great, a Father of the desert.

Abba Anthony said, "He who remains quietly in solitude is saved from three areas of conflict: hearing, speaking and seeing. He only has one remaining area of conflict, the battle in the heart."

Reflection on today's Word.

Where does trouble come from? It must be true that some of the problems in our lives come from outside sources. We can have bad bosses, difficult relatives, and sour friendships. We experience sickness, crime, and accidents. There are natural disasters as well. All of these and more can bring us trouble.

All of these troubles enter our minds through our senses. I only know about them because of what I see, or hear, or touch. These problems come from the outside. In today's Word, Anthony points out that we can avoid many difficulties by shutting our lives away from the outside world. If I never see or hear of the world's tragedies, then they cannot disturb me.

But Anthony isn't providing an easy answer: "retreat from the world and everything will be great for you." Not at all. He goes on to say that just because you aren't being bothered by the outside world, you still have to deal with your own heart. In other words, trouble is unavoidable.

You can't stop problems from happening, but you can go to the God who meets you in your problems. Jesus himself suffered many troubles. He knows what that's like, and he is willing to help you through it.

An action you might take today, in order to put the Word into practice.

What is troubling in your life today? Go to the Lord in prayer with those troubles. Express those to him, and surrender to his will.

Consider today's Bible passage: Jeremiah 17:7-10 (NIV)

Blessed is the one who trusts in the Lord,
   whose confidence is in him.
They will be like a tree planted by the water
   that sends out its roots by the stream.
It does not fear when heat comes;
   its leaves are always green.
It has no worries in a year of drought
   and never fails to bear fruit.
The heart is deceitful above all things and beyond cure.
   Who can understand it?
I the Lord search the heart and examine the mind,
to reward each person according to their conduct,
   according to what their deeds deserve.

Conclude with the Lord's Prayer.

Our Father, who art in heaven,
hallowed be thy Name,
thy kingdom come,
thy will be done,
on earth as it is in heaven.
Give us this day our daily bread.
And forgive us our trespasses,
as we forgive those
who trespass against us.
And lead us not into temptation,
but deliver us from evil.
For thine is the kingdom,
and the power, and the glory,
for ever and ever. Amen.

Tuesday after the Second Sunday in Lent

Begin with a moment of silence.

A Word from John the Short, a Father of the desert.

Abba John the Short said, "If a king wishes to conquer an enemy city, he first cuts off their water and food supply, until perishing with hunger they submit to him. It's the same with our sinful desires. If you accustom yourself to fasting and hunger, the enemy seeking to overcome your soul is weakened."

Reflection on today's Word.

In my religious tradition (I'm an Anglican), we celebrate Christmas and Easter. We don't "celebrate" Lent, though. We "practice" it.

That makes sense. After all, Lent isn't about celebration. It's about suffering, about emptiness, about self-examination. Not much to celebrate there, until it's over on Easter. That's why "practice" is a good word. There's no thought of happiness or sadness associated with that word, not like with the word "celebrate."

Practice doesn't just mean something you do. It means something you do over and over and over again in a controlled setting. If you practice something, you're trying to get good at it. So you might practice piano, for instance, or swinging a baseball bat. You hope to be better at it in the future than you are today. Not because you want to be better at practicing, but so you can get better at performing on the piano, or playing baseball. You're practicing in a controlled setting so that, when the real thing happens, you're ready.

Lent is like that. We give things up, we fast, we pray, we read books like this one, in order to practice suffering in a controlled setting. Our hope is that, when the real thing comes along, we'll be more ready for it.

I once went on a men's retreat. As part of the process, they didn't give us much food. Other men were upset, but I was fine. Why? Because I have practiced fasting. When people I love get sick and die, I have some inner resources to handle my grief. Why? Partially because I have practiced death, through Lent, for many years. That is a benefit of Lent: God forms us into people who are somewhat more able to cope with the difficult things that happen in normal, human life.

An action you might take today, in order to put the Word into practice.

Perhaps you decided to give something up for Lent, but you haven't stuck with it. Make the decision today to recommit to your discipline.

Consider today's Bible passage: 1st Samuel 17:32-36 (NIV)

David said to King Saul, "Let no one lose heart on account of this Philistine; your servant will go and fight him."

Saul replied, "You are not able to go out against this Philistine and fight him; you are only a young man, and he has been a warrior from his youth."

But David said to Saul, "Your servant has been keeping his father's sheep. When a lion or a bear came and carried off a sheep from the flock, I went after it, struck it and rescued the sheep from its mouth. When it turned on me, I seized it by its hair, struck it and killed it. Your servant has killed both the lion and the bear; this uncircumcised Philistine will be like one of them, because he has defied the armies of the living God. The Lord who rescued me from the paw of the lion and the paw of the bear will rescue me from the hand of this Philistine."

Conclude with the Lord's Prayer.

Our Father, who art in heaven,
hallowed be thy Name,
thy kingdom come,
thy will be done,
on earth as it is in heaven.
Give us this day our daily bread.
And forgive us our trespasses,
as we forgive those
who trespass against us.
And lead us not into temptation,
but deliver us from evil.
For thine is the kingdom,
and the power, and the glory,
for ever and ever. Amen.

Wednesday after the Second Sunday in Lent

Begin with a moment of silence.

A Word about an anonymous Brother of the desert.

A disciple was troubled by sexual temptation. He kept on battling and underwent severe fasts for fourteen years, guarding his thoughts and refusing to consent to them. At last he came in to the church and made known to everybody what he had been going through. Everyone fasted for him for a week, joining together in prayer to the Lord, and his temptation ceased.

Reflection on today's Word.

When I was a younger man, I was under the impression that I could handle things on my own. This was sometimes proven by experience. I was competent in a few things, so I could do them without much trouble. I thought I was pretty self-sufficient.

Unfortunately, I didn't yet understand that this wasn't always the case. For instance, I had experienced some trauma in my boyhood. I thought I could just "deal with it." Through depression, poor choices, and the hurt I caused others, came to realize that this wasn't true. There are some things I can't "just deal with." I need help.

The disciple in today's Word thought he could "just deal with" his sexual temptations. Those kind of temptations can be embarrassing. He may have been ashamed of himself, and didn't want anyone else to know what was going on. Finally, though, he humbled himself before God and the church. When he did that, God intervened and granted him relief.

God didn't miraculously heal me of my trauma responses in a single week. However, over years of prayer and counseling, he has helped me integrate my pain into who I am. This healing isn't done, but without my community, I would be in a bad place today. I am grateful that God gave me the grace to reach out when I needed help.

There may be problems that we can confront alone. But most things that really matter are best dealt with in community.

An action you might take today, in order to put the Word into practice.

What do you need help with? Reach out today and ask someone for help with something in your life.

Consider today's Bible passage: James 5:13-16 (NIV)

Is anyone among you in trouble? Let them pray. Is anyone happy? Let them sing songs of praise. Is anyone among you sick? Let them call the elders of the church to pray over them and anoint them with oil in the name of the Lord. And the prayer offered in faith will make the sick person well; the Lord will raise them up. If they have sinned, they will be forgiven. Therefore confess your sins to each other and pray for each other so that you may be healed. The prayer of a righteous person is powerful and effective.

Conclude with the Lord's Prayer.

Our Father, who art in heaven,
hallowed be thy Name,
thy kingdom come,
thy will be done,
on earth as it is in heaven.
Give us this day our daily bread.
And forgive us our trespasses,
as we forgive those
who trespass against us.
And lead us not into temptation,
but deliver us from evil.
For thine is the kingdom,
and the power, and the glory,
for ever and ever. Amen.

Thursday after the Second Sunday in Lent

Begin with a moment of silence.

A Word about a conversation between an anonymous Mother or Father of the desert and our common enemy, Satan.

The Devil once appeared to an abba in the guise of an angel of light and said, "I am the angel Gabriel and I have been sent to you." But the abba said, "Are you sure you weren't sent to someone else? I am not worthy to have an angel sent to me." And the Devil immediately disappeared.

Reflection on today's Word.

This story makes me laugh, which I think is part of its genius. The idea of some old abba of the desert, living alone in a cave, is mystical and serious. Then add the presence of Satan, the incarnation of evil, and I expect there to be some kind of showdown. But there is no showdown; there's no battle. The abba makes a smart-aleck remark and POOF, the Devil is gone.

The humor of the story comes (as humor usually does) from the sense of surprise. Where we expect a battle of wills, instead, we see a holy person who doesn't take themselves seriously. But that shouldn't really be a surprise. Not taking yourself seriously is the very definition of humility. The humble person laughs at herself, points out her own foibles, and knows what a broken person she really is. We might think that a holy person would be very serious about herself, but the opposite is true.

A good way to pay attention to your own spiritual life is to ask the question "Am I willing to laugh at myself?" Can people you live with or work with make gentle fun of you? If someone makes a joke at your expense, how do you react? Not just outwardly, but inside? Being abused isn't God's will for you, and low self-esteem is not God's desire for his children. But neither is a prideful attitude that says, "Yes, I am worthy of an angel visiting me."

An action you might take today, in order to put the Word into practice.

If someone offends you today, take a step back. Are you offended because that person is being mean, or because your pride is injured? If it's the latter, maybe you can laugh at yourself a bit.

Consider today's Bible passage: Romans 12:3 (NIV)

For by the grace given me I say to every one of you: Do not think of yourself more highly than you ought, but rather think of yourself with sober judgment, in accordance with the faith God has distributed to each of you.

Conclude with the Lord's Prayer.

Our Father, who art in heaven,
hallowed be thy Name,
thy kingdom come,
thy will be done,
on earth as it is in heaven.
Give us this day our daily bread.
And forgive us our trespasses,
as we forgive those
who trespass against us.
And lead us not into temptation,
but deliver us from evil.
For thine is the kingdom,
and the power, and the glory,
for ever and ever. Amen.

Friday after the Second Sunday in Lent

Begin with a moment of silence.

A Word from Hyperichius, a Father of the desert.

Abba Hyperichius said, "It's better to be a glutton and drunkard than to devour the life of your brother by slandering him."

Reflection on today's Word.

The desert fathers took the sins of gluttony and drunkenness very seriously, much more seriously than most Christians today. In my church experience, it isn't uncommon to go to a party where fellow Christians overindulge in food and alcohol. No one thinks anything of it. That includes me, especially when it comes to cookies and doughnuts.

The desert monks were different. The *Rule of St. Pachomius*, which many of them followed as a way of defining how to live a holy life, spoke against these sins. *The Rule* said that monks could only eat once a day, and that meal was spare. In some seasons they could only eat every other day. Drinking of alcohol was forbidden most of the time.

That's why this statement by Hyperichius is so extraordinary. Disobeying *The Rule* is bad, but slandering a brother is even worse. Notice his phrase "devour the life." The parallel is striking. Gluttony and drunkenness are about devouring, and so is gossip. In gluttony, I devour food, but in slander, I devour another person. In drunkenness, I feel exhilarated because of alcohol. In gossip, I'm exhilarated because I have brought myself up by tearing someone else down.

I'm sure you've been gossiped about. It's a horrible feeling when I find out I've been slandered. But I still do that to other people, in direct opposition to Jesus' command to "do unto others as you would have them do unto you (Luke 6:31)." Hyperichius encourages us to remember the power of our words. Hurting our bodies is bad enough, but eating up someone else is much worse.

An action you might take today, in order to put the Word into practice.

Today, when you have the opportunity to gossip about someone, say something positive about them instead, or say nothing at all.

Consider today's Bible passage: James 3:2-10 (NIV)

When we put bits into the mouths of horses to make them obey us, we can turn the whole animal. Or take ships as an example. Although they are so large and are driven by strong winds, they are steered by a very small rudder wherever the pilot wants to go. Likewise, the tongue is a small part of the body, but it makes great boasts.

Consider what a great forest is set on fire by a small spark. The tongue also is a fire, a world of evil among the parts of the body. It corrupts the whole body, sets the whole course of one's life on fire, and is itself set on fire by hell.

All kinds of animals, birds, reptiles and sea creatures are being tamed and have been tamed by mankind, but no human being can tame the tongue. It is a restless evil, full of deadly poison. With the tongue we praise our Lord and Father, and with it we curse human beings, who have been made in God's likeness. Out of the same mouth come praise and cursing. My brothers and sisters, this should not be.

Conclude with the Lord's Prayer.

Our Father, who art in heaven,
hallowed be thy Name,
thy kingdom come,
thy will be done,
on earth as it is in heaven.
Give us this day our daily bread.
And forgive us our trespasses,
as we forgive those
who trespass against us.
And lead us not into temptation,
but deliver us from evil.
For thine is the kingdom,
and the power, and the glory,
for ever and ever. Amen.

Saturday after the Second Sunday in Lent

Begin with a moment of silence.

A Word from Sisoe, a Father of the desert.

Abba Sisoe once confidently asserted that for thirty years he had not prayed to God about his sins without saying, "Lord, Jesus, protect me from my own tongue." He said, "but even now, day after day, I fail and transgress because of it."

Reflection on today's Word.

In yesterday's chapter, we read about the danger of the tongue. It's so easy to hurt someone else with what we say. There have a been a few times in my life when just a few words from me have caused a great deal of harm, sometimes to many people.

Sisoe knew this danger, too. That's why whenever he prayed about his sins, he would ask the Lord for help with his tongue. But even though he prayed this way for thirty years, he still found that he sinned every day.

There are two things I want to point out about this. First, I want to say how comforting this is. I know that I sin every day in what I say, and I'm not nearly as holy as Sisoe must have been. If he struggled with this, then I know it's OK that I struggle with it, too. The same God who loved and forgave Sisoe can love and forgive me.

The second thing I notice is how brave Sisoe was. He was willing to tell everyone, to "confidently assert," that he did everything in his power but could not overcome this sin. That might be shaming to some people. But Sisoe, and all the desert Fathers, understood that we are all sinners. We're broken people. We aren't accepted by God because we're good. We're accepted because of what Jesus did for us. So we can boldly and honestly confess our sins, knowing that God values this as an act of humility. Truly owning our failings is far better than covering up our sins.

An action you might take today, in order to put the Word into practice.

What do you need to confess today? Tell the Lord. Even better, also tell a trusted Christian friend and ask for their prayers.

Consider today's Bible passage: 1st John 1:8-10 (NIV)

If we claim to be without sin, we deceive ourselves and the truth is not in us. If we confess our sins, he is faithful and just and will forgive us our sins and purify us from all unrighteousness. If we claim we have not sinned, we make him out to be a liar and his word is not in us.

Conclude with the Lord's Prayer.

Our Father, who art in heaven,
hallowed be thy Name,
thy kingdom come,
thy will be done,
on earth as it is in heaven.
Give us this day our daily bread.
And forgive us our trespasses,
as we forgive those
who trespass against us.
And lead us not into temptation,
but deliver us from evil.
For thine is the kingdom,
and the power, and the glory,
for ever and ever. Amen.

The Third Sunday in Lent

Begin with a moment of silence.

A Word from Arsenius, a Father of the desert.

Abba Arsenius said, "If we seek God, he will appear to us. If we grasp him, he will stay with us."

Reflection on today's Word.

I have an unusual eye condition which requires me to wear hard, weighted contact lenses. These lenses are expensive, but they last for years. Occasionally, while removing one, I'll accidentally drop it. When this happens, I can normally find it quickly. But sometimes, it takes a weird bounce and disappears. So I get down on my hands and knees, searching every inch of the floor. Sometimes this takes a long time. I get nervous, and even scared. But I don't give up because I know for certain that the contact is there somewhere. I always find it.

Searching for God is like that. Sometimes he's easy to spot. He shows up in my life, and I recognize him quickly. Sometimes it seems he isn't there at all, like he wandered off. Sometimes I really need him, but I can't seem to find him. It's in times like those that I think of my contact lens. I know it's there, so I don't give up. I know God is there, at least theoretically, so I don't give up. No matter how scared or angry I get, I can rely on the truth that he exists. I can rely on Jesus' promise that if I seek him, I will find him.

Of course, God is present everywhere. But I don't always, or even often, recognize him. Arsenius must have felt the same way. He sought God, knowing God was always near. More than that, he wanted to grasp God, take hold of him, and make him stay. That part of this Word is beyond my understanding. I don't know how to grasp hold of God. I certainly don't grasp him intellectually, and I've never been able to hold him down. I suppose Arsenius was far more spiritually advanced than I will ever be.

An action you might take today, in order to put the Word into practice.

Spend a few minutes today asking God to reveal himself to you. "Where are you, God?" is a good question to ask him.

Consider today's Bible passage: Luke 11:9-13 (NIV)

Jesus said, "So I say to you: Ask and it will be given to you; seek and you will find; knock and the door will be opened to you. For everyone who asks receives; the one who seeks finds; and to the one who knocks, the door will be opened."

"Which of you fathers, if your son asks for a fish, will give him a snake instead? Or if he asks for an egg, will give him a scorpion? If you then, though you are evil, know how to give good gifts to your children, how much more will your Father in heaven give the Holy Spirit to those who ask him!"

Conclude with the Lord's Prayer.

Our Father, who art in heaven,
hallowed be thy Name,
thy kingdom come,
thy will be done,
on earth as it is in heaven.
Give us this day our daily bread.
And forgive us our trespasses,
as we forgive those
who trespass against us.
And lead us not into temptation,
but deliver us from evil.
For thine is the kingdom,
and the power, and the glory,
for ever and ever. Amen.

Tomorrow is Sunday

Attend a Sunday morning worship service today. Remember that Lent is not something we should do alone, but in the context of community.

Monday after the Third Sunday in Lent

Begin with a moment of silence.

A Word concerning an anonymous Father of the desert.

Someone once asked a certain abba to accept some money for his future needs, but he refused since the work of his hands supplied all his needs. On being pressed repeatedly that at least he might accept something in order to give to the poor, he replied, "There are two reasons why I can't agree. First, I would be taking something I did not need, and second, if I were to give it away, it would only make me conceited."

Reflection on today's Word.

One summer in high school, I got a great job in a restaurant. I call it "great" because they gave me a ton of hours, so I made more money than I had ever seen before. At the same time, I was also attending a little church on Sunday mornings. Near the end of the summer, I thought I should give some of my money to the church. So, I wrote a check my first ever contribution: $100.

For me, that $100 felt like a small fortune. I assumed that the priest would feel the same way. The following Sunday, I went to church fully expecting to get a "thank you" from the pastor. When she didn't say anything, I was offended. I thought at least I'd get a thank-you card in the mail. But nothing. This led me to some anger against the church. Hadn't they seen how self-sacrificial I was? Didn't I deserve some credit?

Of course, I was being immature. I wish I could just chalk it up to my age at the time. Unfortunately, as a pastor, I've encountered a few adults who seem to have the same attitude.

For many of us, giving away money feels good. That's as it should be. In fact, the Bible even says that "God loves a cheerful giver." (2nd Corinthians 9:7). Cheer—happiness—is part of giving. But pride can be part of giving, too. In the case of my teen-aged self, I expected some kind of reward. I didn't give freely. Other people might want to control how the gift is used, or they might want some kind of public recognition. These can all show a heart that isn't giving cheerfully.

I love two things about the abba's Word today. First, he certainly knows his own heart. He's aware of having a difficult relationship with money, and he's honest about his pride. Second, he says that it would be better not to have the money at all than to give it away with a bad attitude. That's a posture I wish more of us Christians had. I'd love for us to be able to give freely, knowing that it isn't money that takes care of us.

An action you might take today, in order to put the Word into practice.

Give some money away. Do it freely and cheerfully.

Consider today's Bible passage: 2 Corinthians 9:6-10 (NIV)

The point is this: whoever sows sparingly will also reap sparingly, and whoever sows bountifully will also reap bountifully. Each one must give as he has decided in his heart, not reluctantly or under compulsion, for God loves a cheerful giver. And God is able to make all grace abound to you, so that having all sufficiency in all things at all times, you may abound in every good work.

As it is written, "He has distributed freely, he has given to the poor; his righteousness endures forever." He who supplies seed to the sower and bread for food will supply and multiply your seed for sowing and increase the harvest of your righteousness.

Conclude with the Lord's Prayer.

Our Father, who art in heaven,
hallowed be thy Name,
thy kingdom come,
thy will be done,
on earth as it is in heaven.
Give us this day our daily bread.
And forgive us our trespasses,
as we forgive those
who trespass against us.
And lead us not into temptation,
but deliver us from evil.
For thine is the kingdom,
and the power, and the glory,
for ever and ever. Amen.

Tuesday after the Third Sunday in Lent

Begin with a moment of silence.

A Word from a conversation between Ammonas and Sisoe, both Fathers of the desert.

Abba Ammonas once said to abba Sisoe, "When I read the Scriptures, I am forever making a sermon out of them in my mind, so that I shall be ready to explain them to whoever asks me about them." Siscoe replied, "There's no need of that. Rather look to simplicity of mind."

Reflection on today's Word.

What is the purpose of reading the Bible? We pastors resonate with Ammonas. It's hard for us to read the Bible without thinking about how to teach it to others. That can be true for lots of Christians. Many of us read the Bible and think of how we're going to use what we've learned in conversations with others. Sometimes, we want to encourage someone else, or bless them. Sometimes, we're looking for ways to win an argument. Maybe we think of the Bible as a textbook or self-help manual. If we can understand it, we can change other people.

Unlike Ammonas, Sisoe favors reading the Bible for the most simple of reasons: to hear from God personally. The purpose of personal Bible reading is to listen to the Lord in order to be transformed by the Holy Spirit. The Bible is frequently hard to understand. It can make us confused, upset, or angry. That's OK. Our primary reason to read it is to allow God to speak. He will say what he needs to say, even when we don't understand everything, even when we can't explain it to others later. God has something to communicate to you in his Word today.

An action you might take today, in order to put the Word into practice.

Read from the Bible today, asking the Lord to reveal himself to you.

Consider today's Bible passage: Hebrews 4:12 (NIV)

For the word of God is alive and active. Sharper than any double-edged sword, it penetrates even to dividing soul and spirit, joints and marrow; it judges the thoughts and attitudes of the heart.

Conclude with the Lord's Prayer.

Wednesday after the Third Sunday in Lent

Begin with a moment of silence.

A Word from an anonymous Mother or Father of the desert.

An abba said, "Although you may be chaste, don't condemn the unchaste, for that is sinning, too. Didn't the same God who said, 'Thou shalt not commit adultery' also say, 'Judge not?'" (9:10)

Reflection on today's Word.

Chastity, abstaining from immoral sexual thoughts or behavior, was part of what it meant to be a monk of the desert. So it would make sense that these same monks would judge those who were unchaste. They might think to themselves, "I'm holy enough not to do that, so that person must not be as holy as I am."

If you're like me, you probably do the same thing. If there's a sin you don't struggle with, you might judge those who commit it. For instance, I don't care about alcohol one way or the other. I'm not tempted to bad drinking behavior. So when I see a friend get drunk, I might judge my friend in my heart.

As this Word points out, that judgment is sin. In fact, it's just as much a sin as being drunk, or unchaste, or any other sin. In a way, judgment is worse than those sins. When I judge, I elevate myself over another human being. I ignore the deep reality of my own sinfulness, and I put myself in the place of God. That sin of pride is the foundation of the some of the most horrible human behavior. Obviously, I can know that unchastity or drunkenness is a sin. I can even talk to my friend about it. But what I should not do is think that I'm better than another person, that I know their heart, or that I wouldn't do the same thing if I were in a similar situation.

An action you might take today, in order to put the Word into practice.

Whom have you judged recently? Instead of judging them, pray for them. Also, pray that the Lord might forgive you for your sin of judgment.

Consider today's Bible passage: Matthew 7:1-5 (NIV)

Jesus said, "Do not judge, or you too will be judged. For in the same way you judge others, you will be judged, and with the measure you use, it will be measured to you."

"Why do you look at the speck of sawdust in your brother's eye and pay no attention to the plank in your own eye? How can you say to your brother, 'Let me take the speck out of your eye,' when all the time there is a plank in your own eye? You hypocrite, first take the plank out of your own eye, and then you will see clearly to remove the speck from your brother's eye."

Conclude with the Lord's Prayer.

Our Father, who art in heaven,
hallowed be thy Name,
thy kingdom come,
thy will be done,
on earth as it is in heaven.
Give us this day our daily bread.
And forgive us our trespasses,
as we forgive those
who trespass against us.
And lead us not into temptation,
but deliver us from evil.
For thine is the kingdom,
and the power, and the glory,
for ever and ever. Amen.

Thursday after the Third Sunday in Lent

Begin with a moment of silence.

A Word from a conversation between Nesteros, a Father of the desert, and one of his disciples.

Abba Nesteros was walking in the desert with a disciple when they saw a large snake and fled. The disciple said to him, "Were you afraid, abba?" "I wasn't afraid, my son," he replied. "But it was a good thing to flee from the sight of the snake since I now have no need to flee from vanity."

Reflection on today's Word.

A few years ago, I was sitting on a riverbank with two of my best friends. We were alone in a national park, relaxing on beach chairs, having a drink. The sun was beginning to set behind the cliffs. Just then, my friend Jim pointed and yelled a word I won't repeat. My other friend Scott and I looked where he was pointing. A long rattlesnake was writhing its way down to the river, not ten feet away from us.

All three of us jumped out of our chairs. Scott and I quickly found rocks and began throwing them at the snake. The snake, for its part, coiled up and began shaking its rattle. We thought we'd scare it away, but it was obvious we had just succeeded in making it angry. Scott and I backed off, throwing rocks as we did. Within a minute, the snake had made its escape, quickly disappearing into the grass farther down the riverbank.

Meanwhile, Jim was back in the car. When we saw him, he rolled down the window and said "Get in." We laughed at him and told him the snake was long gone. Jim wasn't having any of it. "We're leaving."

Scott and I mocked Jim mercilessly. We felt pretty good about ourselves. After all, look how brave we were! But what was really going on? In reality, we were stupid. We could have been killed if we had been bitten by a rattlesnake out there, hours from the nearest hospital. Not only that, but now we were also sinning against Jim. We were filled with arrogance and self-satisfaction, what Nesteros calls "vanity." Jim, on the other hand, was wise. He protected himself, and then protected us by telling us to get in the car.

Scott and I didn't keep our priorities straight. Jim did, even though it cost him some mockery. Think of how common that is in our lives. We do so many foolish things without consideration of who are called to be in Christ. And then, even though we are fools, we congratulate ourselves.

An action you might take today, in order to put the Word into practice.

Ask the Lord to give you wisdom today. When it comes time to make a decision today, even a small one, ask him for his guidance.

Consider today's Bible passage: Proverbs 2:1-8 (NIV)

My son, if you accept my words
    and store up my commands within you,
turning your ear to wisdom
    and applying your heart to understanding—
indeed, if you call out for insight
    and cry aloud for understanding,
and if you look for it as for silver
    and search for it as for hidden treasure,
then you will understand the fear of the Lord
    and find the knowledge of God.
For the Lord gives wisdom;
    from his mouth come knowledge and understanding.
He holds success in store for the upright,
    he is a shield to those whose walk is blameless,
for he guards the course of the just
    and protects the way of his faithful ones.

Conclude with the Lord's Prayer.

Our Father, who art in heaven,
hallowed be thy Name,
thy kingdom come,
thy will be done,
on earth as it is in heaven.
Give us this day our daily bread.
And forgive us our trespasses,
as we forgive those
who trespass against us.
And lead us not into temptation,
but deliver us from evil.
For thine is the kingdom,
and the power, and the glory,
for ever and ever. Amen.

Friday after the Third Sunday in Lent

Begin with a moment of silence.

A Word from Poemen, a Father of the desert.

Abba Poemen said, "It is in temptations that character is made known."

Reflection on today's Word.

One of the Christian spiritual disciplines is the prayer of self-examination. In this prayer, we carefully walk through each of the Ten Commandments and ask difficult questions. We don't just ask "Have I committed murder?" We ask "Have I been reckless, have I hated someone, have my purchases harmed an underpaid salesperson or factory worker?" and other such questions. It's a pretty exhaustive, and exhausting, experience.

Why would anyone do that? For some people, the idea of going through their hearts with a fine-tooth comb would lead only to shame and self-hatred. For others, it might fuel a disorder like OCD or a spiritual sickness called scrupulosity. None of that is good or helpful.

The good purpose of looking closely at my sin is to get a better sense of what triggers me. By that I mean, "What situations, pressures, or habits set me down a road that leads to rebelling against God, hurting myself, or hurting others?" As I get to know my sins, I get to know myself. I also get wisdom about how to live a better life. If I know going into that gym will trigger me to lust, then it's better to avoid that gym. If I know that I'll get drunk and possibly break some laws if I go out with that person, then it's better not to go with them. This isn't, or doesn't have to be, done out of fear. Rather, it can be a way of loving yourself, God, and others by rearranging some simple things in life.

An action you might take today, in order to put the Word into practice.

Consider one sin that you often give into (gossip, rage, sloth, etc.) Prayerfully ask yourself this question: what is one thing that triggers me? Can you avoid that trigger today, with God's help?

Consider today's Bible passage: Luke 21:34-36 (NIV)

Jesus said, "Be careful, or your hearts will be weighed down with carousing, drunkenness and the anxieties of life, and that day will close on you suddenly like a trap. For it will come on all those who live on the face of the whole earth. Be always on the watch, and pray that you may be able to escape all that is about to happen, and that you may be able to stand before the Son of Man."

Conclude with the Lord's Prayer.

Our Father, who art in heaven,
hallowed be thy Name,
thy kingdom come,
thy will be done,
on earth as it is in heaven.
Give us this day our daily bread.
And forgive us our trespasses,
as we forgive those
who trespass against us.
And lead us not into temptation,
but deliver us from evil.
For thine is the kingdom,
and the power, and the glory,
for ever and ever. Amen.

Saturday after the Third Sunday in Lent

Begin with a moment of silence.

A Word from a conversation between a disciple and an anonymous Mother or Father of the desert.

A disciple asked an abba what he should do about the multitude of thoughts which bothered him, because he didn't know how to fight them. The abba said, "Don't fight against all of them, but only against one. All the evil thoughts of a person come from one source. You need to decide which one it is and what it is like, and concentrate on that. The others will then also be beaten down."

Reflection on today's Word.

There is a personality profile that is quite popular right now. It's called the Enneagram. I'm old enough to remember when other profiles were *en vogue*—Myers-Briggs, DISC ... there was even one about colors. These and others have come and gone. I'm confident the Enneagram will, sooner or later, be replaced with something "even better!" Until then, though, it's worth some of your time.

Most personality profiles are based on positive aspects of your personality. "You're an Extrovert, that's great;" "you're a Feeling type, here's why that's good." The Enneagram, on the other hand, is based on your sin (though many people who are into it are not aware of this fact). The fundamental question being asked is this: which of these nine core sins has most formed the way you interact with the world? These core sins are anger, pride, deceit, envy, greed, fear, gluttony, lust, and sloth.

The Word from today's abba is, in a way, telling us to explore the Enneagram. The question she's asking is "what is your fundamental sinful idea?" Her belief is that, if you can figure that out, you can address just that. The other sins, bad thoughts, false ideas, will fall into line.

According to my work with the Enneagram, my central sin is deceit. I have been formed to believe that I have to perform perfectly for everyone. That's how I get my needs met. Since I can't perform perfectly, I will use deceit as a tool to make myself look perfect. I'll either lie about who I am and what I've done, or I'll deceitfully manipulate people to get what I want. At least, that's who I am apart from God's help.

That isn't easy to admit. In many ways, I'd rather have any other flaw. But that's what I got in the lottery of human sinfulness. I have done a great deal of work to overcome that sin. I have put myself in vulnerable and accountable relationships with others. I do what I can to be honest, even and especially when my honesty will hurt me or even hurt others. This doesn't always work, but when I fail I try to be quick to repent and come clean. But, of course, I don't always do that.

My point is that there are sins we are more tempted by than others. By paying attention to that reality, by working through that, we can understand ourselves better. This will, only with God's help, hopefully lead us to become more mature Christians.

An action you might take today, in order to put the Word into practice.

Get online and take an Enneagram assessment. Read about your "number." Does it sound right to you? See if doing some reading about the Enneagram will help you understand and even overcome some of the sin in your life.

Consider today's Bible passage: Galatians 5:19-26 (NIV)

The acts of the flesh are obvious: sexual immorality, impurity and debauchery; idolatry and witchcraft; hatred, discord, jealousy, fits of rage, selfish ambition, dissensions, factions and envy; drunkenness, orgies, and the like. I warn you, as I did before, that those who live like this will not inherit the kingdom of God.

But the fruit of the Spirit is love, joy, peace, forbearance, kindness, goodness, faithfulness, gentleness and self-control. Against such things there is no law. Those who belong to Christ Jesus have crucified the flesh with its passions and desires. Since we live by the Spirit, let us keep in step with the Spirit. Let us not become conceited, provoking and envying each other.

Conclude with the Lord's Prayer.

Our Father, who art in heaven,
hallowed be thy Name,
thy kingdom come,
thy will be done,
on earth as it is in heaven.
Give us this day our daily bread.
And forgive us our trespasses,
as we forgive those
who trespass against us.
And lead us not into temptation,
but deliver us from evil.
For thine is the kingdom,
and the power, and the glory,
for ever and ever. Amen.

The Fourth Sunday in Lent

Begin with a moment of silence.

A Word about Besarion, a Father of the desert.

Someone who had sinned was ordered by the priest to leave the church. Abba Besarion got up and left with him, saying, "I, too, am a sinner."

Reflection on today's Word.

When I was a teenager, I accidentally started a fire that caused significant property damage. It was entirely my fault, and it happened because I was not paying attention when I should have been. Thankfully, no one was injured. On the Sunday that followed the accident, my family and I went to our little church (as we usually did). After service, I overheard my mother relating the incident to some other adults. They were laughing at what happened. I felt that they were laughing at me.

I stormed out of the church building. I couldn't really leave because we had all come together in the family car, so I sat behind some bushes and sulked. I was embarrassed by what I had done. I was angry at my mom and the other adults for laughing at me. But it wasn't just embarrassment and anger; it was shame. Shame is that feeling that there is something deeply wrong with me as a person. One common response to shame is to run away, to hide. That's why I went into the bushes.

The fact that this took place in church, a place where I was supposed to feel close to God, made it worse. It made me feel that my Christian community was rejecting me. Of course, I was overreacting, but that's how I felt.

Unfortunately, churches and other religious organizations sometimes intentionally inflect shame on their members. When someone in the community misbehaves, churches can use shame to punish and, possibly, bring the offender back in line. Pointing out sin is sometimes necessary, of course. But shaming someone, making an example out of them, indicating that they are lesser human beings, is a sin.

In today's Word, Besarion is reacting to another person in his church being shamed. In this case, the unnamed offender is kicked out of the church by the priest because he has sinned in some way. Besarion publicly announces that he will leave the church, too. This must have been embarrassing to the priest because Besarion was a respected religious teacher. But Besarion knew his own sin. Though he was considered a holy man, he knew his own heart. If people weren't allowed to come to church because they were sinners, then Besarion had to leave, too.

Besarion was calling out the hypocrisy of the priest, and all religious people who believe they are not as sinful as other people. The Bible is quite clear: we are all sinners. None of us are perfect. Church is not for perfect people; it's for sinful people. If you are a sinner (like me), then the church is the place for you.

An action you might take today, in order to put the Word into practice.

Attend a church service today. Notice the people who you judge while you're there. Are you a better person than they are? Notice the people who you think might judge you. Are you a worse sinner than they are?

Consider today's Bible passage: 5:29-32 (NIV)

Then Levi held a great banquet for Jesus at his house, and a large crowd of tax collectors and others were eating with them. But the Pharisees and the teachers of the law who belonged to their sect complained to his disciples, "Why do you eat and drink with tax collectors and sinners?" Jesus answered them, "It is not the healthy who need a doctor, but the sick. I have not come to call the righteous, but sinners to repentance."

Conclude with the Lord's Prayer.

Our Father, who art in heaven,
hallowed be thy Name,
thy kingdom come,
thy will be done,
on earth as it is in heaven.
Give us this day our daily bread.
And forgive us our trespasses,
as we forgive those
who trespass against us.
And lead us not into temptation,
but deliver us from evil.
For thine is the kingdom,
and the power, and the glory,
for ever and ever. Amen.

Today is Sunday
Attend a Sunday-morning worship service today. Remember that Lent is not something we should do alone, but in the context of community.

Monday after the Fourth Sunday in Lent

Begin with a moment of silence.

A Word about Theodore and Lucius, both Fathers of the desert.

It was said of Abba Theodore and Abba Lucius of Alexandria that for fifty years they had encouraged each other by saying, "Once the winter is over, we'll leave this place." But when the summer came, they would say, "We'll go once this hot spell is over." This is how they always spoke.

Reflection on today's Word.

On the day after Thanksgiving, 2010, I went for a run. This was highly unusual for me. I am not a sporty person, and I didn't grow up running. But on this day, I was feeling particularly disgusted with myself. So I left the house and just started jogging. I decided I would go as far as I could.

I went a few blocks, and then decided I would stop at the next intersection. When I got to that intersection, I decided I'd keep running until I got to the next one. That happened again, and then again, until I finally looped through my neighborhood and came back home. I got on Google maps and figured out I had run three miles.

From there, I kept going. There were lots of stops and starts, but five years later I ran a marathon. Each time I trained over any distance, I would do what I had done before. I would say to myself "I'll stop at that tree," or "just one more block." But then, when I got there, I'd keep going. Eventually I did that for 26.2 miles.

I found that this kind of self-talk was very helpful. I was breaking up a long, hard task into bite-sized chunks. This is part of 12-step wisdom, too. They like to take their recovery from addiction "one day at a time." The idea is that thinking about "forever" is overwhelming, but you can not use drugs today.

Being a Desert Father must have been incredibly hard. These men and women were isolated, living in environments that barely supported life. They spent all their time either praying or doing tasks that were necessary simply to survive. There wasn't anything glamorous about it.

That's the background to Theodore and Lucius' conversation in our Word. Life was hard for them. So they'd tell each other, "Let's just make it through this month, and then we'll get out of here." They kept on doing this, month after month, for fifty years. While they always spoke of leaving, they never did. They lived out their lives in faithfulness to their calling, their vocation as Fathers of the desert.

You may be going through something difficult right now. It could be something short-term, but it might be a life-long struggle. The Fathers would warn you not to do everything at once. Just do the next right thing, whatever that is. Do that thing and, once you're done, do the next thing. In that way, you can make it through today. And today is the only day you need to confront.

An action you might take today, in order to put the Word into practice.

What is your chief struggle today? With God's help, can you focus on overcoming it just for right now, just for this hour or just for this day?

Consider today's Bible passage: Matthew 6:25-34 (NIV)

Jesus said, "Therefore I tell you, do not worry about your life, what you will eat or drink; or about your body, what you will wear. Is not life more than food, and the body more than clothes? Look at the birds of the air; they do not sow or reap or store away in barns, and yet your heavenly Father feeds them. Are you not much more valuable than they? Can any one of you by worrying add a single hour to your life?

And why do you worry about clothes? See how the flowers of the field grow. They do not labor or spin. Yet I tell you that not even Solomon in all his splendor was dressed like one of these. If that is how God clothes the grass of the field, which is here today and tomorrow is thrown into the fire, will he not much more clothe you—you of little faith?

So do not worry, saying, 'What shall we eat?' or 'What shall we drink?' or 'What shall we wear?' For the pagans run after all these things, and your heavenly Father knows that you need them. But seek first his kingdom and his righteousness, and all these things will be given to you as well. Therefore do not worry about tomorrow, for tomorrow will worry about itself. Each day has enough trouble of its own.

Conclude with the Lord's Prayer.

Tuesday after the Fourth Sunday in Lent

Begin with a moment of silence.

A Word from Syncletica, a Mother of the desert.

Amma Syncletica said, "Just as treasure is soon spent when brought out into the open, so does virtue quickly perish when publicly displayed. Just as wax soon melts when brought to the fire so the soul is weakened by praise and loses its former strength."

Reflection on today's Word.

On January 13th, 2016, someone in Florida won $1.58 billion dollars from the Powerball Lottery. The next day, Teresa Dixon Murray wrote in the *Cleveland Plain Dealer,* "It seems difficult to believe: The lucky winners, possibly three, of Wednesday's $1.5 billion Powerball jackpot will probably go bankrupt within five years." She went on to say, "In fact, about 70 percent of people who win a lottery or get a big windfall actually end up broke in a few years, according to the National Endowment for Financial Education." Ms. Murray's reported that this happens because "lottery winners give away too much money to family and friends."

You can imagine how this happens. Many people who buy lottery tickets are not financially well-off, nor are many of their family and friends. They don't necessarily have the wise counsel and support that wealthy people typically have. But they win the lottery, and suddenly they are rich. Everyone knows it, and people expect the winners to act like they think rich people should act. It doesn't take too long before buying cars, houses, jewelry, and vacations for everyone they know brings even the richest person to the poor house.

Syncletica, who was born into great wealth but gave everything away to the poor, knew this phenomenon. She had probably seen it throughout her life. She also noticed that the same might be said of people who did good deeds. Once their goodness was made public, people treated them differently.

Fame is a strange thing. No matter how someone becomes famous, they often have similar experiences. People come out of the woodwork to become fans, while friends sometimes turn away. These fans fawn over the famous, treating them better than they deserve. But when the fame begins to wane, these fans disappear like morning mist.

Once someone is famous for being good, for being a hero, or for being virtuous, this same thing can happen. The most dangerous thing about this is that the virtuous person begins to believe that they are actually better than other people. This is the easiest way to lose virtue and become a more selfish, critical, and even narcissistic person.

Syncletica's words are a warning to both the famous and the fans. To those who are known for their goodness, it's a stern reminder to abandon pride. To fans, it's a call to remember the broken humanity of even the most heroic people. The only person who won't let us down is Jesus. Everyone else should be treated with respect, but never with worship. Everyone who gets put on a pedestal eventually falls off.

An action you might take today, in order to put the Word into practice.

Who are you putting on a pedestal because you think they are particularly good? Make an effort today to see them as they actually are, as merely human like yourself.

Consider today's Bible passage: Romans 3:20-24 (NIV)

Therefore no one will be declared righteous in God's sight by the works of the law; rather, through the law we become conscious of our sin. But now apart from the law the righteousness of God has been made known, to which the Law and the Prophets testify. This righteousness is given through faith in Jesus Christ to all who believe. There is no difference between Jew and Gentile, for all have sinned and fall short of the glory of God, and all are justified freely by his grace through the redemption that came by Christ Jesus.

Conclude with the Lord's Prayer.

Our Father, who art in heaven,
hallowed be thy Name,
thy kingdom come,
thy will be done,
on earth as it is in heaven.
Give us this day our daily bread.
And forgive us our trespasses,
as we forgive those
who trespass against us.
And lead us not into temptation,
but deliver us from evil.
For thine is the kingdom,
and the power, and the glory,
for ever and ever. Amen.

Wednesday after the Fourth Sunday in Lent

Begin with a moment of silence.

A Word from an anonymous Mother or Father of the desert.

An abba was asked to define humility and said, "it's forgiving your brother from your heart, even before he has apologized."

Reflection on today's Word.

In his great book *Mere Christianity*, C.S. Lewis said, "Do not imagine that if you meet a really humble man he will be what most people call 'humble' nowadays: he will not be a sort of greasy, smarmy person, who is always telling you that, of course, he is nobody."

Humility is not thinking that you are less than everyone else. Rather, humility is thinking correctly of yourself. If you think correctly of yourself, you will notice that you suffer, that you sin and that you have your own hopes and dreams. In this, you are just like everyone else.

In today's Word, our teacher links humility with forgiveness. When you are humble, you see yourself as a sinner. Not a sinner who is worse than everyone, but not one who is better, either. When you see yourself this way, it is much easier to forgive others.

Humility is very much like compassion. You can see the suffering, or the sin, in another and identify with it. You may not have suffered or sinned in the same way. But you know the common humanness of both. Forgiveness comes from the recognition that we are all quite similar.

An action you might take today, in order to put the Word into practice.

Whom do you need to forgive today?

Consider today's Bible passage: Luke 17:3-4 (NIV)

Jesus said, "If your brother or sister sins against you, rebuke them; and if they repent, forgive them. Even if they sin against you seven times in a day and seven times come back to you saying 'I repent,' you must forgive them."

Conclude with the Lord's Prayer.

Thursday after the Fourth Sunday in Lent

Begin with a moment of silence.

A Word from a story about John the Short, a Father of the desert.

Abba John the Short asked the Lord to take away all passions from him, and having become self-confident, he came to a certain abba and said, "Behold a man at peace, with no internal battles." And the abba said, "Go and pray to the Lord that strife may be stirred up in you, for strife nourishes the soul." And when the battlefield began again in his heart he no longer prayed to be delivered from it, but that the Lord might give him the strength to bear it.

Reflection on today's Word.

A friend of mine once had an emergency surgery. At the end of the operation, the surgeon stitched her up. In a couple of days, she was sent home. As you might imagine, she was relieved that the surgery went well, and that everything was going to be OK.

As the days went by, she began to feel that something was wrong in her body. She went back to the hospital. There they discovered that she had an infection underneath the stitches. It was much worse than my friend could have imagined. Even though the wound looked good on the outside, underneath there was something dangerous and deadly.

I expect that all of us want to be at peace. Life is much easier when things are going well, when people like us, and when we aren't anxious. Unfortunately, feeling calm and peaceful is not an indicator that things are good. In fact, peace can be false. In our Word today, John the Short was under the impression that his sense of peace meant he was doing very well in his spiritual life. This was a false belief.

Sometimes we are at peace because we are lying to ourselves. In today's Bible verse, we hear from Jeremiah. In his lifetime, God was going to let a foreign power destroy Jeremiah's homeland because the people had rebelled against God. But the religious leaders were telling everyone not to listen to Jeremiah, that everything would be fine. That would have been like telling my friend not to go back to the hospital. Just because things look doesn't mean that they are good.

Whether we like it or not, it's often conflict that helps us grow. When I am in trouble, I pray a lot more than when I'm not. When I'm scared, I read the Bible, I go to God, I call my friends and ask for help. When I'm feeling fine, I am far less likely to do any of that. You might be the same way.

An action you might take today, in order to put the Word into practice.

Are you willing to ask the Lord to bring more conflict into your life, if it means that he will use this conflict to help you grow?

Consider today's Bible passage: Jeremiah 6:13-15 (NIV)

From the least to the greatest, all are greedy for gain;
　prophets and priests alike, all practice deceit.
They dress the wound of my people as though it were not serious.
'Peace, peace,' they say, when there is no peace.
Are they ashamed of their detestable conduct?
　No, they have no shame at all; they do not even know how to blush.
So they will fall among the fallen;
　they will be brought down when I punish them," says the Lord.

Conclude with the Lord's Prayer.

Our Father, who art in heaven,
hallowed be thy Name,
thy kingdom come,
thy will be done,
on earth as it is in heaven.
Give us this day our daily bread.
And forgive us our trespasses,
as we forgive those
who trespass against us.
And lead us not into temptation,
but deliver us from evil.
For thine is the kingdom,
and the power, and the glory,
for ever and ever. Amen.

Friday after the Fourth Sunday in Lent

Begin with a moment of silence.

A Word from Agathon, a Father of the desert.

Abba Agathon said, "If a wrathful person were to rise the dead, his wrath would still be displeasing to God."

Reflection on today's Word.

Anger is a normal human emotion. Like other emotions, anger is a chemical response in the body. It usually happens in times of threat. God designed us to use our anger to protect the weak, to stop aggressors, to bring justice, and to defend ourselves and those close to us. But, we can use our anger to sin, of course. We can use our anger to serve our selfish desires, our ungodly ambitions, or our self-serving judgement. But even when we misuse it, the anger itself isn't sin.

Wrath, on the other hand, is always sinful for us humans. Wrath isn't about justice; it's about vengeance. It's about destroying other people. Wrath doesn't truly protect anyone, because it will soon harm even those who are most dear to the wrathful person.

Some people feel that they are justified in their wrath. They feel that someone else has done something that deserves destruction. What they don't see is that we all deserve destruction. All of us have rebelled against God, and therefore, all of us deserve his wrath. But, rather than destroying us in his wrath, God accepted our punishment in his own body on the Cross. Jesus turned aside God's righteous wrath by focusing it on himself. This being the case, no human being can judge another to be more deserving of wrath than they themselves are.

Agathon is telling us that wrath is never God's best. In fact, even if the person was so holy that he was able to come back from the dead, God would still reject that person's wrath.

An action you might take today, in order to put the Word into practice.

Do you have wrath against someone else? Are you willing to lay down your wrath, to ask God to forgive you? Are you willing to see the person you hate as someone who deserves as much love as you do?

Consider today's Bible passage: Romans 5:9-11 (NIV)

Since we have now been justified by his blood, how much more shall we be saved from God's wrath through him! For if, while we were God's enemies, we were reconciled to him through the death of his Son, how much more, having been reconciled, shall we be saved through his life! Not only is this so, but we also boast in God through our Lord Jesus Christ, through whom we have now received reconciliation.

Conclude with the Lord's Prayer.

Our Father, who art in heaven,
hallowed be thy Name,
thy kingdom come,
thy will be done,
on earth as it is in heaven.
Give us this day our daily bread.
And forgive us our trespasses,
as we forgive those
who trespass against us.
And lead us not into temptation,
but deliver us from evil.
For thine is the kingdom,
and the power, and the glory,
for ever and ever. Amen.

Saturday after the Fourth Sunday in Lent

Begin with a moment of silence.

A Word from Poemen, a Father of the desert.

Abba Poemen said, "Evil can never drive out evil. If anyone does evil to you, do good to them, for your good deed will destroy their evil ones."

Reflection on today's Word.

Martin Luther King, Jr. said, "The old law of an eye for an eye leaves everybody blind." King was concerned that African-Americans, rightly angered by the violence perpetrated against them by some whites, would respond violently. He felt that this would be a mistake, not only morally but also strategically.

Poemen would have agreed. Like the other Desert Fathers, he lived in a culture of blood feuds. In his time, there was rarely a legal remedy if someone committed a crime against someone else. Instead, the offended person's family would take vengeance on the offender. This would often lead to retribution, and a blood feud would be under way. Some of these feuds lasted for generations, even centuries. There's a sense in which the core conflicts in the Middle East today can be understood as a series of ancient blood feuds.

Poemen, like King, saw that this behavior gets us nowhere. The only way to live a life of peace is to sometimes accept the evil done to us. This isn't fun, and it isn't always possible or even right. Because we live in a nation of laws, we do have the responsibility to report crimes to the police. However, other offenses, more personal evils which are not criminal, can be just as hurtful. In these situations, forgiveness is required. Further, doing acts of good will in response can be powerful ways not only to bless the Lord, but also to cause our adversaries to rethink their actions and, perhaps, repent.

An action you might take today, in order to put the Word into practice.

Consider a wrong that has been committed against you recently. Is there a good deed you can do in response?

Consider today's Bible passage: Romans 12:17-21 (NIV)

Do not repay anyone evil for evil. Be careful to do what is right in the eyes of everyone. If it is possible, as far as it depends on you, live at peace with everyone. Do not take revenge, my dear friends, but leave room for God's wrath, for it is written: "It is mine to avenge; I will repay," says the Lord. On the contrary:
　"If your enemy is hungry, feed him;
　if he is thirsty, give him something to drink.
　In doing this, you will heap burning coals on his head."
Do not be overcome by evil, but overcome evil with good.

Conclude with the Lord's Prayer.

Our Father, who art in heaven,
hallowed be thy Name,
thy kingdom come,
thy will be done,
on earth as it is in heaven.
Give us this day our daily bread.
And forgive us our trespasses,
as we forgive those
who trespass against us.
And lead us not into temptation,
but deliver us from evil.
For thine is the kingdom,
and the power, and the glory,
for ever and ever. Amen.

The Fifth Sunday in Lent

Begin with a moment of silence.

A Word from a Nistero, a Father of the desert.

Abba Nistero said, "Not everyone is given the same work. Scripture tells us that Abraham was given to charity, and God was with him. Elijah sought silence, and God was with him. David was humbled, and God was with him. Do whatever God brings you to, and preserve your heart in peace."

Reflection on today's Word.

I was leading a high-school mission trip in Mexico when I got the phone call. In just a few sentences, I learned that my life would change forever. My wife was calling to tell me two things. First, she had been accepted to one of the best law schools in the country. Second, she was pregnant for the first time.

Laura had wanted to go to law school as long as she could remember. Her reasons for going weren't selfish. She didn't want to get rich or become powerful. She wanted to fight for justice for the poor and marginalized. That's a Christian perspective if I've ever heard one.

The next few weeks were both joyful and agonizing. For complicated reasons, we couldn't move, and the law school was 90 minutes away from our home. So, if Laura went, she'd be a new mom who was spending three hours a day on the road during our baby's first year. She decided, and I agreed, that it wasn't possible. Laura ended up becoming a full-time mother to Ella, and she spent the following years raising our daughters while only occasionally working outside the home.

There we were, the pastor and the stay-at-home mom. So, which one of us was doing God's work? That's the question Poemon addresses in today's Word. His answer? Both of us.

Every Christian is called to a different life and ministry. We may be moms or not, single or married, employed or not, homeless or not. God works through any kind of life. The similarity is that we are all called to serve others with great love. How we do that is up to us as we follow Jesus. Your way of loving others in Christ is different from the way I love others. But neither of us has a superior calling. At best, we are carrying out the call that God put on us when he adopted us as his children.

An action you might take today, in order to put the Word into practice.

Reflect on the ways that you are a blessing to others. Thank God for the ways he uses you.

Consider today's Bible passage: 1st Corinthians 12:12 (NIV)

Just as a body, though one, has many parts, but all its many parts form one body, so it is with Christ. For we were all baptized by one Spirit so as to form one body—whether Jews or Gentiles, slave or free—and we were all given the one Spirit to drink. Even so the body is not made up of one part but of many.

Now if the foot should say, "Because I am not a hand, I do not belong to the body," it would not for that reason stop being part of the body. And if the ear should say, "Because I am not an eye, I do not belong to the body," it would not for that reason stop being part of the body. If the whole body were an eye, where would the sense of hearing be? If the whole body were an ear, where would the sense of smell be? But in fact God has placed the parts in the body, every one of them, just as he wanted them to be. If they were all one part, where would the body be? As it is, there are many parts, but one body.

Conclude with the Lord's Prayer.

Our Father, who art in heaven,
hallowed be thy Name,
thy kingdom come,
thy will be done,
on earth as it is in heaven.
Give us this day our daily bread.
And forgive us our trespasses,
as we forgive those
who trespass against us.
And lead us not into temptation,
but deliver us from evil.
For thine is the kingdom,
and the power, and the glory,
for ever and ever. Amen.

Monday after the Fifth Sunday in Lent

Begin with a moment of silence.

A Word from an anonymous Mother or Father of the desert.

An abba was asked how it was that some people could say that they gazed at the faces of the angels. The abba replied, "It is better to look at your own sins."

Reflection on today's Word.

Recently, I read about a pastor of a large, non-denominational church. On Easter Sunday, he told his congregation that he had recently seen Jesus. He meant literally, saying that they had some sort of face to face conversation.

A number of people in his church, upon hearing the news, shouted "hallelujah" in approval. They put their hands in the air, seeming genuinely moved. And why not? What fantastic news! Jesus is alive and has appeared to someone they know! What Christian has not longed for the same thing: to see Jesus, to have a mystical encounter, to see into heaven, to gaze on the face of the angels?

I obviously don't know if this pastor was telling the truth or not. I'm personally skeptical about it. I do know that many Christians throughout the ages have had supernatural experiences (myself included). We shouldn't take anyone's stories at face value, but neither should we dismiss them out of hand. What we can do is see what fruit these experiences have in a person's life over time.

In the days of the desert Fathers, many disciples had supernatural experiences. In today's passage, someone asks an abba about this. He responds in a surprising way. He says that supernatural experiences are great, but self-examination is better.

Why is that? Surprisingly, supernatural experiences sometimes lead people away from God. They can make the person prideful and arrogant. They can also be false, coming from the person's own mind or even from demons. In that case, the person may believe untrue things that can lead them, and others, into bad places. Many destructive cults have begun when a well-meaning person has a supernatural experience.

Self-examination, on the other hand, leads people to understand themselves more deeply. They see the truth about who they are. They more readily perceive what God is doing with them. They become more humble, while they also see God as more deeply merciful, gracious, and loving than they could have imagined.

An action you might take today, in order to put the Word into practice.

Consider some of the ways you've sinned recently. Ask yourself why you did this. What can your sin show you about yourself? Ask God to forgive you, and know that you are completely forgiven because of the good work of Jesus for you.

Consider today's Bible passage: Ephesians 1:3-8a (NIV)

Praise be to the God and Father of our Lord Jesus Christ, who has blessed us in the heavenly realms with every spiritual blessing in Christ. For he chose us in him before the creation of the world to be holy and blameless in his sight. In love he predestined us for adoption to sonship through Jesus Christ, in accordance with his pleasure and will—to the praise of his glorious grace, which he has freely given us in the One he loves. In him we have redemption through his blood, the forgiveness of sins, in accordance with the riches of God's grace that he lavished on us.

Conclude with the Lord's Prayer.

Our Father, who art in heaven,
hallowed be thy Name,
thy kingdom come,
thy will be done,
on earth as it is in heaven.
Give us this day our daily bread.
And forgive us our trespasses,
as we forgive those
who trespass against us.
And lead us not into temptation,
but deliver us from evil.
For thine is the kingdom,
and the power, and the glory,
for ever and ever. Amen.

Tuesday after the Fifth Sunday in Lent

Begin with a moment of silence.

A Word from Poemon, a Father of the desert.

Abba Poemon said, "One person may seem to live in silence, but in his heart he is constantly condemning others. In reality, he never stops talking. But another who may talk from morning to night in reality has the gift of silence, because he never speaks except to profit his hearers."

Reflection on today's Word.

I was a church youth minister for about eight years. In that time, I got to know a lot of kids who grew up in the church. Most of them had a religion that they had inherited from their parents. It wasn't really theirs yet. They hadn't processed the way the Good News of Jesus impacted them personally. Probably because of this, their understanding of Christianity was that it was essentially about following the rules.

As I got to know them, a teenager would sometimes pull me aside and ask a very important question. They wanted to know how far they could go and have it not "count" as premarital sex. They wanted to follow the rules, but they also wanted to experience sex, and these two were in conflict. They figured that I would have the answer. After all, I was a youth minister.

The problem with this question is that it exposes a fundamental misunderstanding of the Gospel of Jesus. Jesus was primarily interested in a person's heart, with outward actions following from an inner transformation. Legalism, which is typical of adolescent religion, is only interested in what someone does. So, I didn't directly answer their question. Instead, I would address the love of God, the person of Jesus, and what the Holy Spirit was doing in their hearts and lives. This wasn't satisfying, of course, but I hope I was being helpful in the long-term.

We can act in a way that makes people think we are quite pious. We can abstain from the "bad things" in the world, dress ourselves well, and talk like a good person. But that doesn't mean our hearts aren't filled with vile thoughts, hatred, racism, lust, and bitterness.

This is the point Poemon is making in our Word. In his world, silence was a great virtue. But if this virtue was being practiced merely outwardly, what was it worth? How good is it for someone to abstain from sex while their hearts and minds burn with lust? How pleasing is it to God when we hate others in our hearts, even if we keep our opinions to ourselves?

The Holy Spirit is available to us for inner transformation. Only through his miraculous working, with which we participate, can we truly become the people God made us to be. That's why we're on this Lenten journey. We're here to ask for God's help while also abandoning ourselves into his care.

An action you might take today, in order to put the Word into practice.

Ask the Lord to transform your heart today.

Consider today's Bible passage: Mark 7:14-23 (NIV)

Again Jesus called the crowd to him and said, "Listen to me, everyone, and understand this. Nothing outside a person can defile them by going into them. Rather, it is what comes out of a person that defiles them."

After he had left the crowd and entered the house, his disciples asked him about this parable. "Are you so dull?" he asked. "Don't you see that nothing that enters a person from the outside can defile them? For it doesn't go into their heart but into their stomach, and then out of the body." (In saying this, Jesus declared all foods clean.)

He went on: "What comes out of a person is what defiles them. For it is from within, out of a person's heart, that evil thoughts come—sexual immorality, theft, murder, adultery, greed, malice, deceit, lewdness, envy, slander, arrogance and folly. All these evils come from inside and defile a person."

Conclude with the Lord's Prayer.

Our Father, who art in heaven,
hallowed be thy Name,
thy kingdom come,
thy will be done,
on earth as it is in heaven.
Give us this day our daily bread.
And forgive us our trespasses,
as we forgive those
who trespass against us.
And lead us not into temptation,
but deliver us from evil.
For thine is the kingdom,
and the power, and the glory,
for ever and ever. Amen.

Wednesday after the Fifth Sunday in Lent

Begin with a moment of silence.

A Word from Syncletica, a Mother of the desert.

Amma Syncletica said, "Just as a ship cannot be built without nails, so it is impossible for to be saved without humility."

Reflection on today's Word.

In 2004, I was part of a group of people that started a new church. After a great deal of prayer, we decided to name our congregation "Church of the Redeemer." We felt that redemption (being purchased out of slavery) was a great metaphor for the salvation that Jesus Christ offers us.

A few months later, I was driving with a friend who is not a Christian. He didn't grow up in the Church, and was somewhat unfamiliar with our language. He asked me, "What's the name of your church, again?" I told him. He responded, "That's not a good name."

I was a bit taken aback. I wasn't offended, but I was interested in what he meant. So I asked him, "Why not?" "Because," he said, "it implies that people need a redeemer. I don't need one."

When I first read Syncletica's Word, I was put off. I believe what the Christian Reformers taught, that "salvation is by grace alone, in Christ alone, through faith alone." So the idea that we need humility, or any virtue, to be saved irritated me.

But then I thought of that conversation in my car. This man didn't want Jesus' redemption, Jesus' salvation. The reason he didn't want it wasn't because he hated God, or didn't believe that Jesus existed, or anything like that. No, it was because he assumed that he was doing just fine. He didn't need anyone's help. He didn't need to be redeemed, or so he believed.

The sense that I don't need anyone, that I'm fine just as I am under my own power, is pride. It's an elevation of self which I find frankly irrational. If any person takes an honest look at themselves, they will see plenty of faults, imperfections, sins, and even evils. Humility is admitting this reality and recognizing that we need help. We can't save ourselves. In this sense, Syncleteica is right. Unless we are humble enough to know we need Jesus, how can we be saved?

An action you might take today, in order to put the Word into practice.

Admit to God that you cannot save yourself. Ask him to save you, in this life and in the next.

Consider today's Bible passage: Romans 10:9-11 (NIV)

If you declare with your mouth, "Jesus is Lord," and believe in your heart that God raised him from the dead, you will be saved. For it is with your heart that you believe and are justified, and it is with your mouth that you profess your faith and are saved. As Scripture says, "Anyone who believes in him will never be put to shame."

Conclude with the Lord's Prayer.

Our Father, who art in heaven,
hallowed be thy Name,
thy kingdom come,
thy will be done,
on earth as it is in heaven.
Give us this day our daily bread.
And forgive us our trespasses,
as we forgive those
who trespass against us.
And lead us not into temptation,
but deliver us from evil.
For thine is the kingdom,
and the power, and the glory,
for ever and ever. Amen.

Thursday after the Fifth Sunday in Lent

Begin with a moment of silence.

A Word from Poemen, a Father of the desert.

Poemen said, "Suppose there were three people together, and one of them sought to be silent, one was ill but nevertheless gave thanks to God, and a third ministered to others with sincere goodwill. These three are as much alike as if they were all doing the same work."

Reflection on today's Word.

I met Mary Lee when I moved to Nashville in 1999. I was her pastor until she died in 2015. During that entire time, she never sang in the choir. She never served as an usher or minister in a church service. She never sat on the board. I don't recall ever seeing her cooking a meal at church. I don't remember if she ever served on a committee. She never taught a class, or led a small group, or drove the church van.

I met Mary Lee when I moved to Nashville in 1999. Until she died in 2015, other than my wife, she was my greatest prayer warrior. When I didn't know what to do in my ministry, I'd ask for her prayers. When our baby daughter wouldn't go to sleep in a hotel room, Laura and I rang her up in the middle of the night. When I was depressed, she would lift me up to the Lord. I could always count on her prayers.

Mary Lee was as important to the life of our church as any other person, including myself. In failure and success, in peace and in strife, she did an unseen work. My work was obvious, hers was not, but both of us contributed with the gifts God gave us.

According to Poemen, our works are equal. In fact, in the Lord's sight, it's as if we did the same work.

Your work for the Lord is like this, too. Whether your work is prayer, giving, serving the poor, or loving your neighbor, give yourself to that work. Your good work is pleasing to God.

An action you might take today, in order to put the Word into practice.

Whose good work do you need to value more highly? Maybe your own?

Consider today's Bible passage: Matthew 25:14-30 (NIV)

Jesus said, "For it is just like a man about to go on a journey, who called his own slaves and entrusted his possessions to them. To one he gave five talents, to another, two, and to another, one, each according to his own ability; and he went on his journey. Immediately the one who had received the five talents went and traded with them, and gained five more talents. In the same manner the one who had received the two talents gained two more. But he who received the one talent went away, and dug a hole in the ground and hid his master's money.

Now after a long time the master of those slaves came and settled accounts with them. The one who had received the five talents came up and brought five more talents, saying, 'Master, you entrusted five talents to me. See, I have gained five more talents.' His master said to him, 'Well done, good and faithful slave. You were faithful with a few things, I will put you in charge of many things; enter into the joy of your master.'

Also the one who had received the two talents came up and said, 'Master, you entrusted two talents to me. See, I have gained two more talents.' His master said to him, 'Well done, good and faithful slave. You were faithful with a few things, I will put you in charge of many things; enter into the joy of your master.'

And the one also who had received the one talent came up and said, 'Master, I knew you to be a hard man, reaping where you did not sow and gathering where you scattered no seed. And I was afraid, and went away and hid your talent in the ground. See, you have what is yours.'
But his master answered and said to him, 'You wicked, lazy slave, you knew that I reap where I did not sow and gather where I scattered no seed. Then you ought to have put my money in the bank, and on my arrival I would have received my money back with interest. Therefore take away the talent from him, and give it to the one who has the ten talents.'

For to everyone who has, more shall be given, and he will have an abundance; but from the one who does not have, even what he does have shall be taken away. Throw out the worthless slave into the outer darkness; in that place there will be weeping and gnashing of teeth.

Conclude with the Lord's Prayer.

Friday after the Fifth Sunday in Lent

Begin with a moment of silence.

A Word from Poemen, a Father of the desert.

Abba Poemon said, "Have nothing to do with anyone who is always stirring up strife."

Reflection on today's Word.

A friend of mine has a little boy who got into trouble recently. Charlie is a sweetheart, always smiling, with lots of energy. Last month, he started going to a new preschool. In the classroom, there's a child-sized kitchen. The children use it for learning activities, but they can also play during free time. Apparently, Charlie figured out that if you bang the metal pots together, you can make some incredible noises. Probably because he's a natural leader, his fellow students joined him in this behavior. A little-kid-sized riot began, and Charlie was the "instigator."

The world is filled with instigators. Some of them are innocent, like Charlie. Some are heroic, like Nelson Mandela or Martin Luther King, Jr. Some are destructive. When I was in high school, I had a friend who was one of these instigators. Whenever I was with him, you could bet I'd get into trouble. He led me to skip school for the first time, look at pornography for the first time, and steal something serious for the first time.

You probably know an instigator, in the bad sense. Maybe you are one. Instigators bring out our worst selves, but don't make us sin. Unless there's a gun to our heads, we're all responsible for our own behavior. But when we're with them, we find ourselves more angry, more depressed, more judgmental, or more reckless.

Poemon, in his wisdom, suggests that we have nothing to do with such people. Don't misunderstand him. He was fine with the good instigators, the ones who are trying to change the world for good. He was one himself. He's referring to the strife caused by the negative instigators, the ones who help you become the worst version of yourself. They can be a lot of fun, no doubt, but ultimately they aren't helping you in your life in Christ. It's OK to not hang out with that kind of person. Pray for them, love them, but you aren't responsible to remain friends. Who knows; maybe they instigate because you're around, and you aren't good for them, either.

An action you might take today, in order to put the Word into practice.

Do you have a friend who's an instigator of negativity in your life? Are you willing to love that person, pray for them, but start to see less of them?

Consider today's Bible passage: Psalm 1 (NIV)

How blessed is the man who does not walk in the counsel of the wicked, nor stand in the path of sinners, nor sit in the seat of scoffers!

But his delight is in the law of the Lord, and in His law he meditates day and night.

He will be like a tree firmly planted by streams of water, which yields its fruit in its season and its leaf does not wither; and in whatever he does, he prospers.

The wicked are not so, but they are like chaff which the wind drives away.

Therefore the wicked will not stand in the judgment, nor sinners in the assembly of the righteous.

For the Lord knows the way of the righteous, but the way of the wicked will perish.

Conclude with the Lord's Prayer.

Our Father, who art in heaven,
hallowed be thy Name,
thy kingdom come,
thy will be done,
on earth as it is in heaven.
Give us this day our daily bread.
And forgive us our trespasses,
as we forgive those
who trespass against us.
And lead us not into temptation,
but deliver us from evil.
For thine is the kingdom,
and the power, and the glory,
for ever and ever. Amen.

Saturday after the Fifth Sunday in Lent

Begin with a moment of silence.

A Word from Sarah, a Mother of the desert.

Amma Sarah said, "If I were to ask God that everyone should think well of me, I would soon find myself at every person's door having to ask for pardon. Rather, I should pray that my heart becomes pure in all things."

Reflection on today's Word.

A surprisingly high number of my friends are in helping professions. One might argue that all professions are ultimately about helping others, but there are specific jobs that focus on personal care. Nurses, counselors, pastors, social workers, and many others give to others from their hearts every day. While this is a wonderful thing, there is a dark side that comes along with the desire to help: people-pleasing.

People-pleasers are great to be around if you need something. They want to help. They'll even put their own needs aside in order to assist you. People-pleasers might even neglect their friends and families in an effort to make strangers happy. Part of this comes from a sincere concern for others. But it's also motivated by an internal need to be liked, needed, and affirmed.

In our Word, Sarah seems to be a recovering people-pleaser. She knows the temptation to make others like her, and where that temptation leads. If you really want to make everyone like you, then prepare for that to be your full-time job. The task would be endless. To do it perfectly would require that you abandon your humanity and become a walking apology.

Rather than live that way, Sarah decides to go to the Lord in prayer. She knows that a pure heart pleases God, whether or not it pleases anyone else. So she seeks inner transformation over exterior acceptance. Instead of popularity, she chooses to have an audience of One. Only one Person's opinion truly matters.

An action you might take today, in order to put the Word into practice.

Who are you trying to please? Can you take that energy and direct it to prayer today instead?

Consider today's Bible passage: Matthew 6:1-6 (NIV)

Jesus said, "Beware of practicing your righteousness before men to be noticed by them; otherwise you have no reward with your Father who is in heaven. So when you give to the poor, do not sound a trumpet before you, as the hypocrites do in the synagogues and in the streets, so that they may be honored by men. Truly I say to you, they have their reward in full. But when you give to the poor, do not let your left hand know what your right hand is doing, so that your giving will be in secret; and your Father who sees what is done in secret will reward you.

When you pray, you are not to be like the hypocrites; for they love to stand and pray in the synagogues and on the street corners so that they may be seen by men. Truly I say to you, they have their reward in full. But you, when you pray, go into your inner room, close your door and pray to your Father who is in secret, and your Father who sees what is done in secret will reward you."

Conclude with the Lord's Prayer.

Our Father, who art in heaven,
hallowed be thy Name,
thy kingdom come,
thy will be done,
on earth as it is in heaven.
Give us this day our daily bread.
And forgive us our trespasses,
as we forgive those
who trespass against us.
And lead us not into temptation,
but deliver us from evil.
For thine is the kingdom,
and the power, and the glory,
for ever and ever. Amen.

Palm Sunday

Begin with a moment of silence.

A Word from Evagrius, a Father of the desert.

Abba Evagrius told the story of a certain Brother who possessed nothing except a copy of the Gospels, and he even sold that to provide food for the poor. He said, "I have sold the very Word which bade us sell everything and give to the poor."

Reflection on today's Word.

Today is Palm Sunday. On this day, the Church remembers the entrance of Jesus into Jerusalem. He rode on the colt of a donkey, as prophesied in the Old Testament (Zechariah 9:9). The people spread their coats on the road, as well as branches they had cut from the trees. The crowd shouted "Hosanna," which is Hebrew for "save us."

Thus begins the final week in the earthly life of Jesus of Nazareth. Over these seven days, Christ will lay down his life for the sins of the whole world. In one way, this is only something he can do. He alone is God made Man, he alone is perfect, and he alone can atone for our sin. In another way, though, he is an example for all of us. All Christians are called to lay down our lives for the sake of others.

One example of this is found in our Word today. Evagrius encounters a Brother who's sole possession was a Gospel book. In the ancient world, when books had to be hand-made and their contents hand-written, this would have been incredibly valuable. Not only was it valuable from an economic perspective, but also from an educational and spiritual perspective. This book taught the Brother about his Lord. Nothing could be as important.

However, the Brother sold his Gospel book in order to provide food for the poor. Why? Because that very book told him to (Mark 10:21). In this way, he laid down his life. Not his literal life, of course. He didn't die for the poor. But he gave up his most important possession so that others could live through the food he was able to provide.

This Brother gave part of himself away. Jesus gave all of himself away. Each of us are the beneficiaries of the self-giving of both Jesus and countless of our fellow Christians down through the centuries.

An action you might take today, in order to put the Word into practice.

How might you lay down your life for someone today?

Consider today's Bible passage: Mark 11:7-10 (NIV)

The disciples brought the colt to Jesus and put their coats on it; and He sat on it. And many spread their coats in the road, and others spread leafy branches which they had cut from the fields.

Those who went in front and those who followed were shouting:
"Hosanna! Blessed is He who comes in the name of the Lord;
Blessed is the coming kingdom of our father David;
Hosanna in the highest!"

Conclude with the Lord's Prayer.

Our Father, who art in heaven,
hallowed be thy Name,
thy kingdom come,
thy will be done,
on earth as it is in heaven.
Give us this day our daily bread.
And forgive us our trespasses,
as we forgive those
who trespass against us.
And lead us not into temptation,
but deliver us from evil.
For thine is the kingdom,
and the power, and the glory,
for ever and ever. Amen.

Today is Palm Sunday

This is an especially important day to attend a church service. If you don't have a congregation you normally attend, look for one that is having a Palm Sunday procession. You won't regret it.

The Monday of Holy Week

Begin with a moment of silence.

A Word from an anonymous Mother or Father of the desert.

An abba said, "There is no need for a lot of words. Human beings have plenty to say for themselves in these days, but it is deeds which are needed. This is what God wants, not mere words which bear no fruit."

Reflection on today's Word.

A certain man once asked to meet with me. He was raising money for his ministry, and I'm the pastor of a church which gives money to ministries. I already knew him in passing, and we had a few mutual friends. He emailed me some information about his ministry. It looked interesting, so I agreed to get together.

We met up for lunch at one of my favorite places, Baja Burrito. At Baja, you go through a line and tell the servers what you would like on your burrito (there are lots of choices). As this man and I went through the line, I greeted the servers and chatted with them a bit while they assembled my food. This man, on the other hand, snapped orders at them. When one server misunderstood him, he barked at her. She stepped back from the line, obviously shaken.

We sat down with our burritos, and I listed attentively as he told me about all the wonderful things he was doing through his ministry. However, I knew he wasn't going to get a dime from our church. His words were great, but his behavior toward the servers revealed his character. I didn't trust him to minister the Good News to others.

Our Word today reminds us that the world has always been like this. People talk a good game. Important people are valued while the powerless are ignored. We smile when we should, no matter how we feel on the inside. Through social media, we cultivate our images; we're all brand managers for ourselves. We tell people what we want to tell them, doing our best to keep people thinking well of us. Posturing is epidemic in our society.

How do we take today's Word seriously? First and foremost, by asking the Lord to transform us. We can't be good and do good without his gracious help. Our goodness depends on his goodness. Beyond that, we follow him by loving those we encounter. It's easy to love people from a distance. Loving people up close is the hard part, but it's also the call of Christ.

We're called to be intentionally kind to everyone, maybe especially to those who have no power over us. Kindness to servers, cleaners, clerks, and taxi drivers is more valuable to our spiritual transformation than we realize.

An action you might take today, in order to put the Word into practice.

Make an effort today to be kind, especially to those who serve you.

Consider today's Bible passage: James 2:14-18 (NIV)

What good is it, my brothers and sisters, if someone claims to have faith but has no deeds? Can such faith save them? Suppose a brother or a sister is without clothes and daily food. If one of you says to them, "Go in peace; keep warm and well fed," but does nothing about their physical needs, what good is it? In the same way, faith by itself, if it is not accompanied by action, is dead. But someone will say, "You have faith; I have deeds." Show me your faith without deeds, and I will show you my faith by my deeds.

Conclude with the Lord's Prayer.

Our Father, who art in heaven,
hallowed be thy Name,
thy kingdom come,
thy will be done,
on earth as it is in heaven.
Give us this day our daily bread.
And forgive us our trespasses,
as we forgive those
who trespass against us.
And lead us not into temptation,
but deliver us from evil.
For thine is the kingdom,
and the power, and the glory,
for ever and ever. Amen.

The Tuesday of Holy Week

Begin with a moment of silence.

A Word about a conversation between a disciple and St. Anthony the Great, a Father of the desert.

A disciple asked Abba Anthony to pray for him, and he replied, "Neither God nor I can do anything for you unless you yourself take care to cast yourself on his mercy."

Reflection on today's Word.

As long as there have been human civilizations, there have been priests. Sometimes, they've worn feathers and danced around fires. Sometimes, they've stood at stone altars and sacrificed animals. Sometimes, they've worn suits and sat behind their desks as people have cried about their broken marriage. No matter what they look like, or what they're called, we've always had priests.

A priest, by definition, is a person who intercedes to a spiritual being on behalf of humans, most often through a sacrifice. A shaman (witch doctor) enters the spirit world to make it rain. A pagan priestess kills a goat so that Venus will allow a woman to get pregnant. A pastor prays that God will give her parishioner the strength to give up drugs.

Priests can be very helpful, and it makes sense that we want to have them. However, there can be a dark motive for going to a priest; a priest prevents me from having to go to God myself. The priest can make me feel protected from God. I give the priest a chicken, or some money, or a nice compliment, and I hope that the priest will use his holiness to get God to do what I want God to do.

In his Word, Anthony makes it clear that this is now how God works. There is no substitute for going directly to God. Regardless of our situation, God stands ready to receive us. If we're in need, we can go to him. If we have sinned, he is the one who can forgive us. Yes, others can help. But it is only God's power and love that truly matters.

The disciple in this Word wants Anthony to be his priest. But Anthony can't put things right for another person. Also, God won't step in until the disciple casts himself on God's great mercy. The disciple doesn't need a priest. The disciple needs to take an action on his own behalf. Then, God will respond.

An action you might take today, in order to put the Word into practice.

What do you need God's help with today? Tell him that.

Consider today's Bible passage: 1st Timothy 2:2-6 (NIV)

I urge, then, first of all, that petitions, prayers, intercession and thanksgiving be made for all people—for kings and all those in authority, that we may live peaceful and quiet lives in all godliness and holiness. This is good, and pleases God our Savior, who wants all people to be saved and to come to a knowledge of the truth. For there is one God and one mediator between God and mankind, the man Christ Jesus, who gave himself as a ransom for all people.

Conclude with the Lord's Prayer.

Our Father, who art in heaven,
hallowed be thy Name,
thy kingdom come,
thy will be done,
on earth as it is in heaven.
Give us this day our daily bread.
And forgive us our trespasses,
as we forgive those
who trespass against us.
And lead us not into temptation,
but deliver us from evil.
For thine is the kingdom,
and the power, and the glory,
for ever and ever. Amen.

The Wednesday of Holy Week

Begin with a moment of silence.

A Word from Agathon, a Father of the desert.

Abba Agathon said, "I've never willingly gone to sleep bearing a grudge against anyone, nor allowed anyone else to go to sleep holding anything against me."

Reflection on today's Word.

As the pastor of a church, I am called upon to provide counseling for couples. Sometimes this is premarital. Those are usually pretty easy, truth be told. Other times, though, I counsel couples whose relationship has endured several years but is now breaking down. That's not fun for anyone. When I dig into broken relationships, I always find they have one thing in common: resentment.

As couples interact over time, they naturally have conflicts. Some are large, but most are small. Sometimes couples deal with conflict well. They talk things through honestly, and they come to compromises. Often, though, they don't deal with conflict well. One person will dominate another, or one will give in quickly. Sometimes, conflicts are ignored, or brought up much later in order to serve some other argument. Feelings get hurt but never talked about. Forgiveness doesn't happen, leaving hurt and anger. Resentment builds. Eventually, resentment becomes hatred, and hatred collapses into apathy.

This pattern is true of any relationship in which people don't honestly share their feelings and forgive one another. Friends, parents and children, business partners, employers and employees—resentment will kill any meaningful relationship we have.

This is why Agathon's Word is so important. Every day before he slept he would give up his grudges. How does someone do that? There are two main ways. One is to speak to the person who has offended you and work it out. This is not always possible. So the second way is to take the feelings of hurt and anger to the Lord in prayer. In prayer, we can speak forgiveness over someone whom we cannot speak to, even someone who is dead.

Does this always make us feel better? No, not immediately. But over time, we'll find that speaking forgiveness (and seeking forgiveness from God for our own sins) eventually leads to less and less resentment.

Agathon also wants us to confess our sins to those we've sinned against. This is also something that can't always be done, or can't be done face-to-face. If it can be done, it should be. I seem to have made a regular habit of confessing to my wife, children, friends, and colleagues. It isn't fun, but it does help me walk in the way of Christ. And, hopefully, it helps others not hold resentment against me.

Finally, we should confess to the Lord the ways we have harmed others, and we should seek God's forgiveness. In this way, we're reminded that we're just as sinful as everyone else. The people who hurt us aren't worse than us. That knowledge can help us to lay down our resentments, as well as to have compassion on those who harm us.

An action you might take today, in order to put the Word into practice.

Whose forgiveness do you need to seek today?

Consider today's Bible passage: Ephesians 4:25-27, 31-32 (NIV)

Therefore each of you must put off falsehood and speak truthfully to your neighbor, for we are all members of one body. "In your anger do not sin:" Do not let the sun go down while you are still angry, and do not give the devil a foothold. ... Get rid of all bitterness, rage and anger, brawling and slander, along with every form of malice. Be kind and compassionate to one another, forgiving each other, just as in Christ God forgave you.

Conclude with the Lord's Prayer.

Our Father, who art in heaven,
hallowed be thy Name,
thy kingdom come,
thy will be done,
on earth as it is in heaven.
Give us this day our daily bread.
And forgive us our trespasses,
as we forgive those
who trespass against us.
And lead us not into temptation,
but deliver us from evil.
For thine is the kingdom,
and the power, and the glory,
for ever and ever. Amen.

The Thursday of Holy Week

Begin with a moment of silence.

A Word from an anonymous Mother or Father of the desert.

An abba said, "We shall not be condemned because our thoughts are evil, but only if we make evil use of them. Through our thoughts we can either suffer shipwreck or be crowned with glory."

Reflection on today's Word.

Sometimes, I feel like there is a little man in my head whose entire job is to criticize anyone he sees. When I walk into a restaurant, or drive down the street, or even come into church, the little man evaluates people, especially people I don't know, and lets me know instantly what he thinks. "That guy's cool" or "that child is so cute" are some of his statements. Other times I get "put some clothes on!" or "that guy's dangerous" or a sarcastic "nice shirt."

Of course, that little man is me. I am quick to evaluate, to categorize, and to judge. Those are my thoughts, and there is nothing I can do about them. I am powerless over those initial reactions. However, I'm not powerless over what happens next. That's what the abba is telling us today.

I can't control my initial thoughts, but I can decide what to do with them. I can choose to speak them, or to keep them silent. I can decide to act on an impulse, or to keep it contained. I can decide to run with my initial reaction, or to reconsider it.

Reconsidering an initial reaction is an especially powerful thing. If I see someone and judge them as unworthy in some way, the best thing I can do next is to ask myself, "Why did I think that?", and then to honestly evaluate my thought. Where did that idea come from? What prejudice did that thought reveal? What would God say about this person? That usually causes me to pray, to ask God's forgiveness, and to look to him for transformation.

My thoughts don't control me—unless I let them. Of course, there have been many times when I've thought something, acted on it, and caused harm to myself and others. I know what that's like, and I bet you do too. But we don't have to live like that. Of course, we will have wicked thoughts. But we can take these to the Lord. We can learn from them. And we can allow the Holy Spirit to transform us so that we develop a more Christ-like character.

An action you might take today, in order to put the Word into practice.

Notice an unkind thought you have about someone today. Ask God and yourself that question, "Why did I think that?"

Consider today's Bible passage: Luke 6:36-38 (NIV)

Jesus said, "Be merciful, just as your Father is merciful. Do not judge, and you will not be judged. Do not condemn, and you will not be condemned. Forgive, and you will be forgiven. Give, and it will be given to you. A good measure, pressed down, shaken together and running over, will be poured into your lap. For with the measure you use, it will be measured to you."

Conclude with the Lord's Prayer.

Our Father, who art in heaven,
hallowed be thy Name,
thy kingdom come,
thy will be done,
on earth as it is in heaven.
Give us this day our daily bread.
And forgive us our trespasses,
as we forgive those
who trespass against us.
And lead us not into temptation,
but deliver us from evil.
For thine is the kingdom,
and the power, and the glory,
for ever and ever. Amen.

Good Friday

Begin with a moment of silence.

A Word from Poemen, a Father of the desert.

As Abba Poemen was traveling in Egypt, he saw a woman sitting by a gravestone weeping so bitterly that he said, "All the pleasures in the whole world would not be able to outweigh this poor soul's grief. So ought the disciple always to let compunction dwell in his heart."

Reflection on today's Word.

Today is Good Friday, the day the Church sets aside to relive the crucifixion of Jesus. Notice I say "relive," not simply "remember." Remembering Jesus' sacrifice is a daily discipline of the Church. On this day, we choose to enter into that sacrifice by reliving it.

Congregations do this in many ways. One might have a candlelight service of quiet songs. Another might show a film. Another might walk the Stations of the Cross, following a large, wooden cross through fourteen different events of that first Good Friday. Still other churches might have times of meditation, silence, readings, or communion. Regardless of how it's done, the purpose is the same: to gaze upon the Son of God hanging on a tree for our sins.

The saints of the Church have taught that we should meditate on the crucified Jesus, either by looking at an artistic representation or by seeing him in our imaginations. As we look at Jesus, we're urged to confess the ways in which we nailed him to that tree. This isn't literal, of course. But if Christ is crucified for our sins, then it's our sin (those evils done and those good things left undone) that have, in part, placed him there. This is a powerful form of meditation, and one that is especially appropriate for this day.

When we confess our sins in this way, we hope that "compunction will dwell in our hearts," as Poemen says. Compunction is the distress we feel when we're aware of our wrongdoings. Poemen compares this distress to that of a woman weeping by the grave of her beloved. Compunction, like grief, is an inner pain that can hurt as much as any physical wound. But, like grief, compunction isn't an end to itself.

Compunction is not God's way to punish us, nor can we pay God back for our sins by feeling sorrow. Rather, the purpose of compunction is to lead us to a deeper sense of God's love and forgiveness. Christ's sacrifice on the cross is the punishment for our sins. He has borne the responsibility for us. Our compunction rightly leads to gratitude and even joy.

BALANCED MEAL
CHIEF (Dalmatian).—
Hannah Taylor, Kannapolis, NC

23·Saturday
March *2019*

TALL STACK
CHARLIE (Lab mix).—
Dr. Chelsea Ballinger, Greenville, IL

24·Sunday
March *2019*

When we downplay or ignore our sins, we downplay God's goodness. When we focus too much on our sins or seek to pay God back, we also downplay God's goodness. But when we look our sin in the face, feel it, and then release it to the Lord, we open ourselves to deeper Christian maturity.

An action you might take today, in order to put the Word into practice.

Meditate on the Cross of Christ today. Either spend time with an image of the crucifixion, or imagine it. Sit in silence and ask the Lord to give you a true sense of what Jesus did for you.

Consider today's Bible passage: Mark 15:16-39 (NIV)

The soldiers led Jesus away into the palace (that is, the Praetorium) and called together the whole company of soldiers. They put a purple robe on him, then twisted together a crown of thorns and set it on him. And they began to call out to him, "Hail, king of the Jews!" Again and again they struck him on the head with a staff and spit on him. Falling on their knees, they paid homage to him. And when they had mocked him, they took off the purple robe and put his own clothes on him. Then they led him out to crucify him.

A certain man from Cyrene, Simon, the father of Alexander and Rufus, was passing by on his way in from the country, and they forced him to carry the cross. They brought Jesus to the place called Golgotha (which means "the place of the skull"). Then they offered him wine mixed with myrrh, but he did not take it. And they crucified him. Dividing up his clothes, they cast lots to see what each would get.

It was nine in the morning when they crucified him. The written notice of the charge against him read: the king of the Jews. They crucified two rebels with him, one on his right and one on his left. Those who passed by hurled insults at him, shaking their heads and saying, "So! You who are going to destroy the temple and build it in three days, come down from the cross and save yourself!" In the same way the chief priests and the teachers of the law mocked him among themselves. "He saved others," they said, "but he can't save himself! Let this Messiah, this king of Israel, come down now from the cross, that we may see and believe." Those crucified with him also heaped insults on him.

At noon, darkness came over the whole land until three in the afternoon. And at three in the afternoon Jesus cried out in a loud voice, "Eloi, Eloi, lema sabachthani?" (which means "My God, my God, why have you forsaken me?").

When some of those standing near heard this, they said, "Listen, he's calling Elijah." Someone ran, filled a sponge with wine vinegar, put it on a staff, and offered it to Jesus to drink. "Now leave him alone. Let's see if Elijah comes to take him down," he said.

With a loud cry, Jesus breathed his last. The curtain of the temple was torn in two from top to bottom. And when the centurion, who stood there in front of Jesus, saw how he died, he said, "Surely this man was the Son of God!"

Conclude with the Lord's Prayer.

Our Father, who art in heaven,
hallowed be thy Name,
thy kingdom come,
thy will be done,
on earth as it is in heaven.
Give us this day our daily bread.
And forgive us our trespasses,
as we forgive those
who trespass against us.
And lead us not into temptation,
but deliver us from evil.
For thine is the kingdom,
and the power, and the glory,
for ever and ever. Amen.

Holy Saturday

Begin with a moment of silence.

A Word from Evagrius, a hermit of the desert.

Evagrius said, "A monk was told of the death of his father. He replied to the messenger, 'Don't be blasphemous. My Father cannot die.'"

Reflection on today's Word.

According to the Church's historical understanding of the Gospels, Jesus died on a Friday and was raised to life again the following Sunday morning. Therefore Holy Saturday, today, is the day we sit in the reality that Jesus Christ, God made flesh, was truly dead.

This is a great mystery. What does that mean? What was the universe like on that day? We can't know, of course. But this is the day to remember that God himself went to the place that we all must go, to the place of the dead. He entered into our greatest fear.

In today's Word from Evagrius, we get a twist on this idea. The monk is told of the death of his earthly father, but he reminds the messenger that his true Father is God. God lives forever, and so his Father is immortal. This is a reminder that bad things happen, even to holy people like this monk. Fathers die, mothers die; spouses and siblings and friends and even children die. Eventually, you will die. Death is common to all of humanity.

The good news is that God died. Because he died, he knows what it's like. He experienced the death of loved ones, and eventually, he experienced his own death. He has taken on death in order to become the "firstborn from the dead" (Revelation 1:5, NIV).

And the monk is right. His Father has immortal life. And so does the Son of the Father. Jesus has immortal life. So, yes, today we remember his death. But tomorrow we'll remember his resurrection. His death was temporary; his resurrection is eternal. And our deaths, and the deaths of those we love, are similar. We die temporarily. But because of what Jesus has done, we will rise to eternal life. We will be with him, and all his beloved ones, forever.

An action you might take today, in order to put the Word into practice.

Make today a day of rest.

Consider today's Bible passage: Revelation 1:4b-8 (NIV)

Grace and peace to you from him who is, and who was, and who is to come, and from the seven spirits before his throne, and from Jesus Christ, who is the faithful witness, the firstborn from the dead, and the ruler of the kings of the earth.

To him who loves us and has freed us from our sins by his blood, and has made us to be a kingdom and priests to serve his God and Father—to him be glory and power for ever and ever! Amen.

"Look, he is coming with the clouds,"
    and "every eye will see him,
even those who pierced him;"
    and all peoples on earth "will mourn because of him."
So shall it be! Amen.

"I am the Alpha and the Omega," says the Lord God, "who is, and who was, and who is to come, the Almighty."

Conclude with the Lord's Prayer.

Our Father, who art in heaven,
hallowed be thy Name,
thy kingdom come,
thy will be done,
on earth as it is in heaven.
Give us this day our daily bread.
And forgive us our trespasses,
as we forgive those
who trespass against us.
And lead us not into temptation,
but deliver us from evil.
For thine is the kingdom,
and the power, and the glory,
for ever and ever. Amen.

Easter Sunday

Begin with a moment of silence.

A Word from St. Anthony the Great, a Father of the desert.

Abba Antony said, "I no longer fear God, I love him, for love has driven out fear."

Reflection on today's Word.

Today is Easter Sunday, the day we celebrate the Resurrection of Jesus. Today is a day of joy and feasting, and the beginning of fifty days of celebrating the triumph of Christ over the dead.

On this day, you might reflect back on your Lenten journey. It's possible that you didn't read this book every single day, even though you had intended to. It's likely you didn't do each of the actions I suggested, or keep your fast, or do some of the other good things you had hoped to do. The best way I can address you in this is to step out of the way and give the last word to St. John Chrysostom. He was a contemporary of the later Desert Fathers, and is widely considered the greatest preacher in Christian history. His Easter sermon is particularly well known, and I offer a portion of it to you now.

> Are there any who are devout lovers of God?
> Let them enjoy this beautiful bright festival!
> Are there any who are grateful servants?
> Let them rejoice and enter into the joy of their Lord!
> Are there any weary from fasting?
> Let them now receive their due…
> Let us all enter into the joy of the Lord!
> First and last alike, receive your reward.
> Rich and poor, rejoice together!
> Conscientious and lazy, celebrate the day!
> You who have kept the fast, and you who have not,
> rejoice, this day, for the table is bountifully spread!
> Feast royally, for the calf is fatted.
> Let no one go away hungry.
> Partake, all, of the banquet of faith.
> Enjoy the bounty of the Lord's goodness!
> Let no one grieve being poor,
> for the universal reign has been revealed.
> Let no one lament persistent failings,
> for forgiveness has risen from the grave.
> Let no one fear death,
> for the death of our Savior has set us free…

For Christ, having risen from the dead,
is become the first-fruits of those who have fallen asleep.
To Christ be glory and power forever and ever. Amen!

An action you might take today, in order to put the Word into practice.

Attend a church service. Celebrate Jesus! Feast, relax, and have a good time. Your Lent is over.

Consider today's Bible passage: John 20:11-18 (NIV)

Now Mary Magdalene stood outside the tomb crying. As she wept, she bent over to look into the tomb and saw two angels in white, seated where Jesus' body had been, one at the head and the other at the foot. They asked her, "Woman, why are you crying?"

"They have taken my Lord away," she said, "and I don't know where they have put him." At this, she turned around and saw Jesus standing there, but she did not realize that it was Jesus. He asked her, "Woman, why are you crying? Who is it you are looking for?"

Thinking he was the gardener, she said, "Sir, if you have carried him away, tell me where you have put him, and I will get him."

Jesus said to her, "Mary." She turned toward him and cried out in Aramaic, "Rabboni!" (which means "Teacher").

Jesus said, "Do not hold on to me, for I have not yet ascended to the Father. Go instead to my brothers and tell them, 'I am ascending to my Father and your Father, to my God and your God.'"

Mary Magdalene went to the disciples with the news: "I have seen the Lord!" And she told them that he had said these things to her.

Conclude with the Lord's Prayer.

Bibliography

If you want to explore the Desert Fathers more fully, here are some books you might be interested in.

Andrew of Crete. *The Life of our Holy Mother Mary of Egypt.* Public Domain.

Athanasius the Great. *The Life of Saint Anthony.* Public Domain.

Carrigan Jr., Henry L. *The Wisdom of the Desert Fathers and Mothers.* Paraclete Essentials.

Forbes, F. A. *Saint Athanasius The Father of Orthodoxy.* Public Domain.

Gregory of Tours. *Vitae Patrum.* Public Domain.

Hannay, James O. *The Wisdom of the Desert.* Public Domain.

Lane, Belden C. *The Solace of Fierce Landscapes: Exploring Desert and Mountain Spirituality Exploring Desert and Mountain Spirituality.* Oxford University Press.

Merton, Thomas. *The Wisdom of the Desert.* New Directions.

Nouwen, Henri J. M. *The Way of the Heart: The Spirituality of the Desert Fathers and Mothers.* HarperCollins Christian.

Pachomius. *The Rules of Pachomius.* Public Domain.

Palladius. *The Lausiac History.* Public Domain

Pseudo-Athanasius. *The Life and Regimen of the Blessed and Holy Syncletica.* Public Domain.

Ward, Benedicta. *The Desert Fathers: Sayings of the Early Christian Monks.* Penguin Classics.

.

About the Author

The Reverend Thomas McKenzie lives in Nashville with his wife, Laura. Together, they have two college-aged children. He's the author of *The Anglican Way: A Guidebook*. He's written or edited smaller works as well, including a devotional guide to Advent entitled *The Harpooner*.

Thomas was born and raised near Amarillo, Texas. His Bachelor's degree is from the University of Texas at Austin, and his Master's Degree in Divinity is from Trinity School for Ministry in Ambridge, Pennsylvania.

Thomas is a priest of the Anglican Church in North America and the Anglican Diocese of Pittsburgh. He's the founding pastor of Church of the Redeemer in Nashville, Tennessee. He's an oblate of the Monastery of Christ in the Desert in Abiquiu, New Mexico.

You can stay in contact with him at www.ThomasMcKenzie.com

Made in the USA
Columbia, SC
21 March 2019